COMING
The LATTER
RAIN

COMING
The LATTER
RAIN

ARE YOU READY?
ARE YOU SURE?

THOMAS A. DAVIS

5685 Parsons Road, Wildersville, Tennessee 38388

Orion Publishing wishes to acknowledge the assistance of J. Philip Wiygul D.D.S., M.S., in the publication of this book.

Proofread by Lorrie Dana and Paulette Hodges
Copy edited by Rose Heinrich
Cover design and layout by Richard Ramont
Copy layout by Michael Prewitt

Orion Publishing, Wildersville, TN 38388.

ISBN 0-9659327-1-0

Contents

Introduction

This book is about the work of the Spirit upon the heart. It is about conviction of sin, "and of righteousness, and of judgment" (John 16:8). It is about appeals and warnings, and help and encouragement. It is about the Spirit dwelling in the heart providing power for holy living.

It is also about the response of the human heart to the moving of the Spirit. This book deals with resistance and unbelief, stubbornness and pride, anger and resentment, temptation and defeat, repentance, faith, and surrender, freedom and victory, the transformed life, and the fruit-bearing life. It is about falling down and getting up again. In short, it is about life as the Christian, or would-be-Christian, often finds it.

Actually, in essence, this book has more to do with the former rain than the latter rain. What I am really discussing in these pages is the *preparation* for the latter rain found in an appropriate response to the former rain. So the present volume is about the latter rain from the perspective of being ready for it when it comes. The former rain as an absolute prerequisite to receiving the latter rain.

We are inclined to emphasize the latter rain, and with good reason. But we need to accentuate the early rain far more than we do. "Unless the early showers have done their work, the latter rain can bring no seed to perfection."[1]

Ellen White warns us that the latter rain may be falling on hearts all around us, and we might not even recognize it,[2] to say nothing of being ready to receive it. So, while this book includes an important chapter on the latter rain, this volume is not simply a discussion of the events and experiences associated with it. Much more importantly, it has to do with heart preparation for its reception, which, of course, has to do with the early rain. Thus, I have contoured this volume around the concept of the former rain, God's efforts to make us ready for the latter rain and translation, and our response, at various stages, to His efforts. The book is in three parts. The first part has two chapters, one on the condition of the Laodicean church as described by the Bible and the Spirit of Prophecy. The second chapter is a discussion of the latter rain.

The second part is in six "phases" composed of pairs of parallel chapters in a pattern of initiative and response. God takes the initiative, always. The first move is of necessity His. We respond, in one manner or another, to His initiative. The success of each move God makes depends upon our response. If our response is affirmative, He can go on to the next step. If it is negative, God is limited in what He can do for us. For you and I are creatures of free will.

"The Spirit taketh the things of God, just as fast as the soul resolves and acts in accordance with the light revealed."[3] Progress, then, depends upon you and me.

At the same time God's part is infinitely more important than ours. As Ellen White points out, "The part man is required to sustain is immeasurably small, yet in the plan of God it is just that part that is needed to make the work a success."[4]

"The work of the Holy Spirit is immeasurably great."[5]

"Immeasurably inferior is the part which the human agent sustains; but if he is linked with the divinity of Christ, he can do all things through the strength that Christ imparts."[6] In the world of today the Seventh-day Adventist Church desperately needs the Holy Spirit. First, He must be in the life of each individual member, and that is *you and I.* Then the Spirit must be urgently present in the efforts that are made to win others to the truth. "All human effort combined is weakness without the deep moving of the Spirit of God. . . . Without His help the deep learning and restless energy of a Paul, the eloquence and talent of an Apollos, will fall infinitely short of convicting and bringing one soul to repentance [It may bring people to baptism]. . . . [However] while man can do nothing without God, the Lord would do nothing without the human channel."[7]

While the justification for this work, the letter to the Laodiceans and the Spirit of Prophecy writings, is addressed to the church as a whole, this book is intended to speak in a more specific sense to the individual church member.

For the most part the chapters of this book, especially those of the second section, are interdependent, one linking with, and leading into, the next. So it is recommended that they be read in sequence.

Except as noted, the texts used throughout this book are from the New King James Bible.

1. White, Ellen G., *Testimonies to Ministers,* page 506.
2. Ibid., page 507.
3. White, Letter 135, 1898.
4. White, *God's Amazing Grace,* page 319.
5. White, *Review and Herald,* November 29, 1892.
6. White, *Christ's Object Lessons,* page 82.
7. White, Letter 85, 1898.

The work of gaining salvation is one of copartnership, a joint operation. There is to be co-operation between God and the repentant sinner (*The Acts of the Apostles,* page 482).

Keep on working with fear and trembling to complete your salvation, because God is always as work in you to make you willing and able to obey His own purpose (Philippians 2:12, TEV).

Lord, You will establish peace for us, for *You* have also done all *our* works *in* us (Isaiah 26:12, NKJV). [Italics supplied.]

There is but one power that can bring us into conformity to the likeness of Christ, that can make us steadfast and keep us constant. It is the grace of God that comes to us through obedience to the law of God (*My Life Today,* page 100).

PART ONE

Chapter 1

For People Serious about the Latter Rain

People who become really serious about a matter prove their seriousness by being willing to face up to some things they may not have been disposed to confront previously.

This book is for that kind of people.

Serious Seventh-day Adventists are interested in the latter rain. What they know about it tells them that an unprecedented power will come with its reception, a power that will "lighten the whole earth with [its] glory" and "miracles will be wrought, the sick will be healed, and signs and wonders will follow the believers."[1]

We desire this power. We know that we need it, desperately. We want to have victory over our sins. We want to see "the work" finished. We want to "go home." We have been on this sin-afflicted planet long enough and to spare. We want to see a period put on the whole sin experiment.

Perhaps many of us are frustrated about the deferral of the latter rain, the coming of which we may believe will solve the problems implied above. Sometimes we ask ourselves questions such as this: If the latter rain is to do the great work necessary to prepare us for Jesus' coming, why have we not received it? Why does God allow us to stumble along in our sins if the latter rain will cure that problem? If the latter rain will make it possible to wind up human affairs in a burst of glory and victory, why does God delay that experience, and allow the terrible, seemingly unhindered, march of sin to continue across our groaning planet?

Then we remember the Spirit of Prophecy exhortation to pray for the latter rain.[2] And so sometimes the pastor calls his local congregation, and sometimes our world leaders call the world church, to engage in earnest prayer that God will bestow upon His people that coveted gift.

But is sincere prayer all that is needed to bring the latter rain? Is the Laodicean church in such a healthy spiritual condition that all that is required for God to pour out His Spirit is that we, like Elijah at Carmel, pray for it in faith long enough and persistently enough?

"What Shall We Do?"

Or is there need for us to ponder the formula Peter offered on another occasion when, in great seriousness, and in the context of another spiritual downpour—Pentecost—the question was asked, "Men and brethren, what shall we do?" (Acts 2:37).

Peter's response? *"Repent* therefore and be converted, that your sins may be blotted out, so that times of refreshing may come from the presence of the Lord" (Acts 3:19).

Relating the experience of the disciples in preparation for Pentecost, the inspired pen wrote,

> It was by the confession and forsaking of sin, by earnest prayer and consecration of themselves to God, that the early disciples prepared for the outpouring of the Holy Spirit on the Day of Pentecost. *The same work, only in greater degree, must be done now.*[3] [Italics supplied.]

What this is telling us is that Peter and John and Nathaniel and Matthew became seriously interested in an experience that is associated with the early rain. By this they prepared for the tongues of fire, and they would not have received those tongues had they not done so.

Thus, people serious about the latter rain will also be serious about the former rain without which they cannot receive the latter rain.

Note that prayer was only part of the formula that brought Pentecost. There was also the confessing and forsaking of sin, and "consecration of themselves to God." And we may be assured that these were not carried out casually, formally, simply because it was "the thing to do." For the disciples,

> These days of preparation were days of deep heart searching. [They] felt their spiritual need and cried to the Lord for the holy unction that was to fit them for the work of soul saving.[4]

A. W. Tozer probably did not understand the latter rain as clearly as Seventh-day Adventists do. But he wrote,

I long for the positive and genuine renewal which would come if the Will of God could be totally accomplished in our lives. Everything that is unspiritual would flee, and all that is not Christlike would vanish, and all that is not according to the New Testament would be rejected.

If this ever happens, it will come because Christians are finally willing to look on the Savior and let Him work, and each will take his own cross with such gladness that he can breathe, "Oh cross, oh good cross, I embrace thee."[5]

Do we not need a spiritual ardor and depth of commitment such as A. W. Tozer describes here?

A Need for Spiritual Realism

Unless every dimension of body, soul, and spirit is involved in that preparation, we shall continue spinning our wheels in our Christian experience. If that involvement is not our experience, we shall not be prepared, or be able to prepare, for the latter rain, until we are individually realistic about our spiritual condition, and set about to seriously seek the Lord in this matter.

In discussing this subject it may not be easy to find a balance in which the seriousness of the message is plain, and yet its presentation does not appear judgmental and discouraging. It may require a fine balance to reach an equilibrium between Pollyanna optimism and pessimistic extremism. But I wonder whether, when all is considered, the greater danger is not in the direction of optimism, for we humans are very prone to grasp any excuse that promises to rescue us from seeing ourselves in a bad light. Thus we fail to comprehend the dangers which we might at least view from the other end of the spectrum.

But while we must seek for balance, it is essential that we see the Laodicean condition—which is described as the general condition of the last church (Revelation 3:14–22)—as a serious condition applying to us as a church and as individuals, and as an impediment to the latter rain. And we must decidedly do something about it.

Are We Listening?

On the basis of the biblical characterization of the Laodiceans, one might suspect that of all the two-thousand-year history of the Christian church, their condition is the most exasperating for God. According to Revelation 3, in no other church has God had to deal with a people quite like the Laodiceans. Of no other church except Sardis has He been unable to find a word of commendation.

The Laodicean syndrome may be seen as the most frustrating because it is the most difficult to reach, and people in that condition are the most difficult to persuade of their sad and terribly dangerous state.

Note the almost irreconcilably different perspective the lukewarm Laodiceans have of themselves from that which the True Witness has of them:

> I am rich, I have prospered, and I need nothing; . . . You are wretched, pitiable, poor, blind, and naked (Revelation 3:17, RSV).

God is trying to speak to us; are we really listening?

In the words of Jesus, "If ever you were willing to listen, listen now!" (Matthew 11:15, TLB).

Do the Bible and Spirit of Prophecy's Characterizations Still Apply?

In taking up this matter of the Laodiceans, one of our problems is, Does the description of the Laodicean church in Revelation 3 really apply to the church today? And to what degree do Ellen White's characterizations apply, one hundred years, more or less, after she penned them? We must agree that obviously many things have changed since her time.

As Seventh-day Adventists, most of us accept the historicist approach that, as symbols, the seven churches represent seven periods of the church, reaching down to the end of time. This means that Laodicea, the seventh, is the last church existing before Jesus returns.

The biblical depiction still applies, then, because there is no other church period to follow. And we have no reason to insist that the general description Ellen White gives of the Laodiceans does not also still apply. As David Newman, former editor of *Ministry* magazine, pointed out:

> Ellen White . . . during the course of her ministry never encouraged the church to consider that it had escaped from [the] Laodicean condition. She said we would never do the work that God really wants us to do until we wholeheartedly admit that

we are in a Laodicean condition and seek the divine remedies as our priority.

So we now need to realistically face up to the fact that, if we are the Laodiceans, we must accept not only the name, but must seriously receive the perturbing biblical description of the Laodiceans as applying to us as a church, and so to us as individuals.

But while we admit we are Laodiceans, ironically we help confirm it by the very fact that, after so admitting, we seem blind to the very implications of that admission. Which tends to verify that, in the majority, we "do not know" that we are "wretched, miserable, poor, blind, and naked" (Revelation 3:17).

In 1882 Ellen White, writing of the situation in the church, stated that "many think far too favorably of the present time."[6] We doubt that a lot of spiritually perceptive people among us would seriously insist conditions are more favorable in the church now than then.

> If ever there was a people that needed to heed the counsel of the True Witness to the Laodicean church to be zealous and to repent before God, it is the people who have had opened up before them the stupendous truths for this time, and who have not lived up to their high privileges and responsibilities.[7]

Here's a statement that I find somewhat scary.

> You [the Laodicean church] may manifest great zeal in missionary effort, and yet because it is corrupted with selfishness, and tastes strongly of self, it is nought in the sight of God; for it is a tainted, corrupted offering.[8]

This was written in 1882. But can we discount this evaluation today? Are we purer of motive than the church of 1882? Are our efforts at worldwide evangelism today tainted with secret desires for self or denominational exaltation?

In 1894 Ellen White stated that the Laodicean message "is highly applicable to us as a people." It "reveals our condition as a people."[9] (We must recognize that it does not apply to *all* Seventh-day Adventists, *all* professed Christians, because always some respond to the message, open the heart's door, and welcome the Savior. See *Testimonies for the Church,* Volume 2, page 217. But the majority are lukewarm. "The greater part are lukewarm professors, having a name but no zeal."[10])

In addition to being lukewarm, Laodicea is described as suffering from other spiritual maladies.

Laodicean Characteristics

The Laodiceans are characterized as being self-satisfied. Of that church Ellen White writes,

> Christ sees that which man does not see. He . . . cannot take up the names of those who are satisfied in their own self-sufficiency. He cannot importune in behalf of a people who feel no need of His help, who claim to know and possess everything.[11]

It has been said that "A man does not have to be unfaithful to his wife or dishonest in his dealings, or anti-social in any way in order to be a sinner. He has only to be satisfied with himself."

It is important to note it is not the kinds of sins referred to in this statement for which the Laodiceans are indicted. Rather, it is for sins of the heart, sins of motive and attitude.

The Laodiceans are described as being in an unrepentant state.

> "Be zealous and repent" (Revelation 3:19).

> Christ sees that which man does not see. He sees the sins which, if not repented of, will exhaust the patience[12] of a long-suffering God.[13]

The Laodiceans are pictured as having Christ outside the heart.

> "Behold, I stand at the door and knock. If anyone hears My voice and opens the door, I will come in. . . ." (Revelation 3:20).

> All must obtain a living experience for themselves; they must have Christ enshrined in the heart, His Spirit controlling the affections, or their profession of faith is of no value, and their condition will be even worse than if they had never heard the truth.[14]

The Laodiceans are characterized as lacking the work of grace in the life.

12

The internal work of grace is wanting in their hearts.[15]

This lack is associated with the eye salve, which the Laodiceans are counseled to buy.

> The eye salve is that wisdom and grace which enables us to discern between the evil and the good, and to detect sin under any guise.[16]

The Laodiceans, we are told, are spiritually naked.

> I counsel you to buy from Me ... white garments to clothe you and to keep the shame of your nakedness from being seen (Revelation 3:18, RSV).

> What is it that constitutes the wretchedness, the nakedness of those who feel rich and increased with goods?—It is the want of the righteousness of Christ. In their own righteousness they are represented as clothed with filthy rags, and yet in this condition they flatter themselves that they are clothed upon with Christ's righteousness.[17]

The Laodiceans are in a condition of near spiritual blindness.

While they are "not entirely blind,"[18] they are in a state in which they are unable to discern their spiritual imperfections and deficiencies. Unless they buy the eye salve that they might see clearly, their state can but progress into total blindness.

Any one of these conditions, persistently maintained, is enough to obligate Jesus to finally reject lukewarm Laodiceans.

But Are Things Really That Bad?

It is extremely difficult for us to put ourselves and the "greater part" of the church in the above picture. Not that we do not recognize that there are problems among us, some of which are serious. Nevertheless, in our hearts we may be inclined to feel the picture has been painted with too dark colors, laid on too thickly; that surely things are not as bad as described here. After all, *we* are part of Laodicea, and we *know* the people who compose Laodicea. Can they really, and fairly, be described in those terms?

The above characterizations may truly describe the Israelites of old, we reason, or the church in Ellen White's generation. But the church of which we are a part? Emotionally, we probably have difficulty making the application.

We may therefore at times be inclined to be somewhat hard on people who emphasize these problems. We may characterize them as critical or even troublemakers, which, indeed, some may be.

But we dare not allow our own subjective conclusions or emotional reactions to shut out the voice of the True Witness. By so doing we may be putting ourselves where the Holy Spirit cannot reach us as He must.

> The testimony, so cutting and severe, cannot be a mistake, for it is the True Witness who speaks, and His testimony must be correct.[19]

There is a grave lesson for us in the experience of the church of Laodicea in Asia, as described in the Spirit of Prophecy.

> Much excellent labor was bestowed upon the Laodicean church. To them was given the exhortation, "Be ye therefore perfect, even as your Father which is in heaven is perfect." But the church did not follow up the work begun by God's messengers. They heard, but they failed to appropriate the truth to themselves, and to carry out the instruction given them. The result that followed is the result always sure to follow the rejection of the Lord's warnings and entreaties.[20]

In His loving concern and desire to save us Laodiceans, God places these things on record. Shall we not heed and respond?

The Latter Rain is for Laodiceans

While the condition of the Laodiceans is clearly serious, it is not hopeless. The fact that Christ appeals to us to "buy" tells us something can be done. There is hope for the Laodiceans. In fact, *the latter rain is going to fall on Laodiceans!*

> The counsel of the True Witness does not represent those who are lukewarm as in a hopeless case. There is yet a chance to remedy their state, and the Laodicean message is full of encouragement; for the backslidden church may yet buy the gold of faith and love, may yet have the white robe of the righteous-

ness of Christ. . . . There is hope for our churches *if they will heed the message given to the Laodiceans.*[21] [Italics supplied.]

(At this point we must remind ourselves that Laodicea does not mean "lukewarm," as is commonly thought, but "a people judged." We are Laodiceans because we live in the period of the final judging. Those living just before Christ returns who, through Him, meet the test of the judgment, will receive the latter rain. There is a solemn motivation in the Laodicean message.)

So what is to be done?

It is easier to lay plans, promote projects, and work in the hope of bringing the blessing and finishing the work, than to face up to the daunting spiritual problems implied in the Laodicean message. But we must also realize that until we do correct this condition, all our appeals, plans, protestations, promotions, and efforts, will be without the desired result. "We cannot depend upon form or external machinery" to bring the latter rain.[22] Without a serious willingness to do something about our Laodicean predicament, even our prayers will be of no avail.

Denial Comes Naturally

While reading the descriptions of the church quoted above, which church of course is made up of individuals—you and me—denial might come naturally. But anyone who candidly ponders the Laodicean message, and examines the general condition of the church today, will not hide his head in the sand by denying that we fit the description.

Possibly we fit it more closely today than did the church of Sister White's day.

> It is difficult for us to understand ourselves, to have a correct knowledge of our own characters. The word of God is plain, but often there is an error in applying it to one's self. There is liability to self-deception and to think its warnings and reproofs do not mean me. "The heart is deceitful above all things, and desperately wicked: who can know it?" Self-flattery may be construed into Christian emotion and zeal. Self-love and confidence may give us assurance that we are right when we are far from meeting the requirements of God's word.[23]

In closing this chapter I am going to make a final point about which I ask your indulgence if it is off the mark. But I am sometimes confused as to just what to think about our church. In this chapter we have reviewed just a little of what Ellen White has to say about the Laodicean church, the Seventh-day Adventist Church. I believe it applies to us today at least as much as it did to the church of her day. And we can hardly say that her words are flattering. To the contrary. Hopeful, yes. Supportive, yes. But hardly complimentary.

Then I sometimes listen to Sabbath morning or camp meeting sermons that assure us that, although yes, there are problems in the church, nevertheless we in the congregations are generally fine, that our condition is such that we may have an assurance of salvation, and that we need only believe more fervently that God accepts us. And I wonder, are the Spirit of Prophecy writings, and the sermons I am hearing, about the same church? Were Ellen White and the True Witness mistaken after all? Or is the situation like that which D. Martyn Lloyd-Jones described in telling of his own pre-conversion experience in the churches he attended: "The preaching we had was always based on the assumption that we were all Christians, that we would not have been there in the congregation unless we were Christians."[24] And is such an assumption among us a reason why we hear, or read, so little about the need of the new birth among Seventh-day Adventists?

Somehow, I feel I must choose to give credence to the inspired pen about our situation. While of the two choices it may be the considerably less comfortable, it still has more authority, to my mind. I don't know about you.

In this context, let me close by reminding you of the sentence with which we started this chapter: People who become really serious about a matter prove their seriousness by being willing to face up to some things they may not have been disposed to confront previously.

1. White, *The Great Controversy,* pages 611, 612.
2. White, *Testimonies to Ministers,* page 509.
3. Ibid., page 507.
4. White, *The Acts of the Apostles,* page 37.
5. Tozer, A. W., *I Talk Back to the Devil,* (Harrisburg, PA: Christian Publications, Inc., ©1982), page 90.
6. White, *Testimonies for the Church,* Volume 5, page 80.
7. White, *Review and Herald,* June 4, 1889.
8. White, *Seventh-day Adventist Bible Commentary,* Volume 7, page 961.
9. Ibid.
10. White, *Testimonies for the Church,* Volume 4, page 87.

11. White, *Review and Herald,* July 23, 1889.
12. That God is patient does not indicate that the objects of His patience are in a saving relationship with Him. In His longsuffering He is hoping they will repent so that He can forgive, cleanse, and save them.
13. White, *Seventh-day Adventist Bible Commentary,* Volume 7, page 964.
14. White, *Testimonies for the Church,* Volume 5, page 619.
15. White, *Testimonies for the* Church, Volume 4, page 88.
16. Ibid.
17. White, *Review and Herald,* August 7, 1894.
18. White, *Review and Herald,* November 23, 1897.
19. White, *Testimonies for the Church,* Volume 3, page 253.
20. White, *Seventh-day Adventist Bible Commentary,* Volume 7, page 964.
21. Ibid., page 966.
22. White, *Testimonies to Ministers,* page 512.
23. White, *Testimonies for the Church,* Volume 5, page 332.
24. Lloyd-Jones, D. Martyn; quoted by C. Raymond Holmes, "Holiness: By What Authority?" in *Journal of the Adventist Theological Society,* Volume 5, Number 1, pages 3, 4; as quoted by Iain H. Murray, in *D. Martyn Lloyd-Jones: The First Forty Years,* (Edinburgh: The Banner of Truth Trust, ©1982), page 59.

Chapter 2
The Latter Rain: What? When? Where? Why? Who? How?

I have some vivid memories of rainy seasons in the tropical countries in which we have lived. I can still visualize the rain being hurled by driving winds against the flapping canvas awnings dropped down like outside curtains over the windows to keep the water from spraying into our house in the Philippines, and can hear the torrent's furious drumming on the side and roof of our bungalow.

I can remember the weeks leading up to the monsoons in India. By the time the rains were expected the fields were sunbaked, fissured, apparently lifeless.

In India the monsoon rains start in the south and gradually spread north up the subcontinent like a great, gray curtain. When the time approaches for them to begin the people further north are alert for tidings of their progress. Will the rains be on time? Will they fall long enough? Will they be sufficient?

These are almost life and death questions for many, because their lives often virtually depend on the answers. And when the rains finally come, there is celebration. I have seen people stand out in the first rain and luxuriate in it as we would in our bathroom showers.

Likewise in Palestine, the people were dependent upon the rainy season for the sustaining of life itself. When Moses warned the Israelites of the results of disobedience to God he said, "The Lord will smite you with . . . drought. . . .And the heavens over your head shall be brass, and the earth under you shall be iron" (Deuteronomy 28:22, 23, RSV). A severe drought could make the land unlivable.

In Bible times the Israelites understood that the rains, like everything else in nature, were controlled by God. He gave as He saw fit. In the theocracy obedience and cooperation brought rains, disobedience and rebellion could result in drought (Deuteronomy 11:13, 14; 28:15, 24).

We must remember that all these things were "written for our admonition" (1 Corinthians 10:11).

In Palestine the rainy season is from late October or early November to late March or early April. Rain does not fall at other times of the year. So what is called the early rain in the Bible comes in the autumn, and makes plowing and sowing possible. The latter rain comes in the spring, at the end of the wet season, and matures the grain for the harvest. The rains are referred to by Hosea as symbolizing a work done by the Lord. "Let us know, let us pursue the knowledge of the Lord. . . . He will come to us like the rain, like the latter and former rain to the earth" (Hosea 6:3; see also 2 Samuel 23:2–4).

The Spiritual Application

This spiritual meaning, while perhaps alluded to by other Old Testament writers (Isaiah 44:3; Joel 2:28, 29), is not further developed in the Bible. We go to the Spirit of Prophecy for that.

"The outpouring of the Spirit in the days of the apostles," writes Ellen White, "was the beginning of the early, or former, rain, and glorious was the result." She continues, "To the end of time the presence of the Spirit is to abide with the true church."[1]

When the Spirit was poured out at Pentecost—in a singular endowment of special power—it did not end there. The Spirit would be with the church right down to the end of time.

Applying the lesson to the church—as the former rain was to facilitate plowing and sowing, and the rains kept on through the rainy season for the continued growth of the grains—so the Spirit is with His people throughout all remaining time for the spiritual development of God's people. *But unless we individually are continually receiving of that spiritual rain, we shall not have developed sufficiently to receive of the latter rain.*

> Unless the former rain has fallen, there will be no life; the green blade will not spring up. Unless the early showers have done their work, the latter rain can bring no seed to perfection.[2]

Did we read that statement rather mechanically? Let's look at it again. Unless the grain has received enough moisture through the growing period to bring it to a certain stage of development by the time of the last rains of the season, those rains will do the grain no good, for a certain growth is essential for the grain to be matured for the harvest by those final rains. So, unless the Holy Spirit, day by day, moment by moment, is able to carry on a work of development in our hearts and lives so that we are becoming more and more like Jesus, we are in danger of not being spiritually advanced enough to be benefited by, and therefore to receive, the latter rain.

> The ripening of the grain represents the completion of the work of God's grace in the soul. By the power of the Holy Spirit the moral image of God is to be perfected in the character. We are to be wholly transformed into the likeness of Christ.[3]

When Shall We Receive the Latter Rain?

A question of great importance to Seventh-day Adventists is, When is the latter rain to be poured out?

Ellen White gave an answer to this question about a hundred years ago. In 1897 she wrote,

> It *is* the time of the latter rain, when the Lord will give largely of His Spirit.[4] [Italics supplied.]

This statement has been a source of puzzlement for some. If the time of the latter rain had arrived one hundred years ago, where is that rain? Obviously, it has not fallen, for the impressive and dramatic events predicted for that time have not taken place.

> Servants of God, with their faces lighted up and shining with holy consecration, will hasten from place to place to proclaim the message from heaven. By thousands of voices, all over the earth, the warning will be given. Miracles will be wrought, the sick will be healed, and signs and wonders will follow the believers.[5]

The writer goes on to tell us that the light will penetrate everywhere; and neither church, family, nor any other type of obstacle will hold multitudes from accepting truth. This has not been fulfilled since 1897; it is not being fulfilled now.

But, again we remind ourselves, Ellen White said, in 1897, that it *is* the time of the latter rain. How are we to understand this?

My years in the tropics helped me to see an answer. There, as in the Holy Land, there is a certain time when the rains are expected. We have seen that in Palestine they normally begin sometime around the end of October or the beginning of November. In India they are expected in June and last through October.

But the rains do not always come at the expected time. Sometimes they are several weeks late, which is an occasion for considerable anxiety in the nation. So, even though, in India, in June it *is* the time for the monsoons to bring the rains, for some reason sometimes they do not arrive on schedule.

Very likely the Indian farmer does not understand the basis of the delay, although a meteorologist may. The farmer knows only that the rains have not come, and that consequently his crops are endangered.

It *is* the time of the latter rain. You and I are living in that time. The church has been in the time of the latter rain for many long years. But there has been a delay—a long delay. Why? One reason is that God Himself will choose the hour and circumstances for the outpouring of the latter rain.

There are times when we may feel that surely things are ripe in the church for the outpouring, but it doesn't happen.

> The circumstances may seem to be favorable for a rich outpouring of the showers of grace. But God Himself must command the rain to fall.[6]

Another reason found in the Spirit of Prophecy writings places the burden squarely upon the church itself.

> For forty years did unbelief, murmuring, and rebellion shut out ancient Israel from the land of Canaan. The same sins have delayed the entrance of modern Israel into the heavenly Canaan. In neither case were the promises of God at fault. It is the unbelief, the worldliness, unconsecration, and strife among the Lord's professed people that have kept us in this world of sin and sorrow so many years.[7]

> *When* the laborers have an abiding Christ in their own souls, when all selfishness is dead, when there is no rivalry, no strife for the supremacy, when oneness exists, when they sanctify themselves, so that love for one another is seen and felt, *then* the showers of the grace of the Holy Spirit will just as surely

come upon them as that God's promise will never fail in one jot or tittle. But when the work of others is discounted, that the workers may show their own superiority, they prove that their own work does not bear the signature it should. God cannot bless them.[8] [Italics supplied.]

The question is sometimes asked, "Why, if we have the truth, do we not see a greater manifestation of the Spirit of God?" God cannot reveal Himself till those who profess to be Christians are doers of His word in their private lives, till there is oneness with Christ, a sanctification of body, soul, and spirit. Then they will be fit temples for the indwelling of the Holy Spirit.[9]

Surely these words should move each one of us candidly to pray in the sentiment of Psalm 139:23, 24: "Search me, O God, and know my heart: try me, and know my thoughts: and see if there be any wicked way in me, and lead me in the way everlasting" (KJV).

The Purpose and Message of the Latter Rain

What is the purpose of the latter rain? A statement in *Maranatha* (page 170) tells us the purpose. It also helps us to put a time tag on the question, When will the latter rain be poured out? by describing conditions prevailing when it will come.

It will be poured out just prior to the close of probation, shortly before the seven last plagues fall on humanity. The nations will be in great turbulence, ready to burst forth in uncontrolled fury, but will be supernaturally restrained so that the final work of the gospel can be completed.

"At that time," we are told, "the 'latter rain,' or refreshing from the presence of the Lord, will come."

Then we are given the purpose of the latter rain: 1) *"to give power to the loud voice of the third angel, and"* 2) *"prepare the saints to stand in the period when the seven last plagues shall be poured out."* [Italics supplied.]

By the latter rain, "they are prepared for the trying hour before them."[10] It is also described as preparing "the church for the coming of the Son of man."[11]

The latter rain and the loud voice of the third angel are synonymous, as we learn from *Early Writings,* page 271.

23

We are told the substance of the message that will be given under latter-rain power in *Testimonies to Ministers,* page 92. It is the same message presented in 1888. It is "justification through faith in the Surety." It will invite men and women "to receive the righteousness of Christ, which is made manifest in obedience to all the commandments of God." This, we are told, "is the third angel's message, which is to be proclaimed with a loud voice, and attended with the outpouring of His Spirit in a large measure." This message, "the message of the renewing power of God's grace will be carried to every country and clime, until the truth shall belt the world."[12]

"A Terrible Mistake"

We have quoted three reasons Ellen White has offered for the bestowal of the latter rain. One of them requires our particular attention: "to prepare the saints to stand in the period when the seven last plagues shall be poured out."

These words are sometimes understood as meaning that—no matter that the spiritual condition of Seventh-day Adventists may be casual or indifferent—those who are to go through the seven last plagues will be given the latter rain to prepare them in a special way for that time. They may have been lax in their Christian living, may have known they should be more earnest, more zealous, in their Christian experience. They have put those things off. But the latter rain will take care of that. It will "zap" them into a spiritual experience they have neglected to acquire before.

Those who think this "are making a terrible mistake." "Many have in a great measure failed to receive the former rain." The latter rain does not bring a miraculous spiritual experience to men and women who have not, in their daily lives "obtained all the benefits that God has provided for them."[13]

This matter merits a number of statements from the Spirit of Prophecy writings to drive the idea home.

> We must not wait for the latter rain. It is coming upon all who will recognize and appropriate the dew and showers of grace that fall upon us [now].[14]

> We may be sure that when the Holy Spirit is poured out *those who did not receive and appreciate the early rain* will not see or understand the value of the latter rain.[15] [Italics supplied.]

Those who make no decided effort, but simply wait for the Holy Spirit to compel them to action, will perish in darkness.[16]

I saw that many were neglecting the preparation so needful and were looking to the time of "refreshing" and the "latter rain" to fit them to stand in the day of the Lord and to live in His sight. Oh, how many I saw in the time of trouble without a shelter! They had neglected the needful preparation; therefore they could not receive the refreshing that all must have to fit them to live in the sight of a holy God.[17]

I was shown God's people waiting for some change to take place—a compelling power to take hold of them. But they will be disappointed, for they are wrong. They must act, they must take hold of the work themselves and earnestly cry to God for a true knowledge of themselves. . . . The harvest of the earth is nearly ripe.[18]

Are we looking forward to the latter rain, confidently hoping for a better day, when the church shall be endued with power from on high and thus fitted for work? The latter rain will never refresh and invigorate the indolent, who do not use the powers God has given them.[19]

Thus, when we read that one purpose of the latter rain is to "prepare the saints to stand in the period when the seven last plagues are poured out," it means a people already *spiritually* prepared by the Holy Spirit. They have settled "into the truth, both intellectually and spiritually, so they cannot be moved."[20] These will be given a faith commensurate with the need, and a holy determination, and a fortitude that makes it possible to go through that fearsome period. It will not be possible for us to survive that time except as we have that preparation.

In this context we note that it is "the latter rain which revives and strengthens them [God's people] to pass through the time of trouble."[21]

So the latter rain is not to bring a miraculous spiritual experience to those who did not have an intimate, growing, relationship with Jesus before.

We may be sure that when the Holy Spirit is poured out those who did not receive and appreciate the early rain will not see or understand the value of the latter rain.[22]

The Latter Rain *Will* Come

> Throughout our churches there is to be a reconversion, and a reconsecration to service.
>
> . . . Floods of spiritual power are now to be poured forth upon those prepared to receive it.[23]

That latter rain is coming suddenly, the inspired pen tells us, and with ten times more power than accompanied the preaching of the Midnight Cry in 1844.[24]

> The entire church, acting as one, blending in perfect union, is to be a living, active missionary agency, moved and controlled by the Holy Spirit.[25]

We cannot know all the reasons for the delay of the latter rain. God, in His inscrutable wisdom, has reasons we probably could not even understand. But we can understand our part in causing the delay. And we can do something about it.

> Today you are to give yourselves to God, that He may make of you vessels unto honor, and meet for His service. Today you are to give yourself to God, that you may be emptied of self, emptied of envy, jealousy, evil surmising, strife, everything that shall be dishonoring to God. Today you are to have your vessel purified that it may be ready for the heavenly dew, ready for the showers of the latter rain; for the latter rain will come, and the blessing of God will fill every soul that is purified from every defilement.[26]
>
> When we bring our hearts into unity with Christ, and our lives into harmony with His work, the Spirit that fell on the disciples on the day of Pentecost will fall on us.[27]

The following sobering statement reinforces the concept that if we are not readying our souls hour by hour, the latter rain will avail us nothing. It first makes an uncompromising declaration about what is necessary that we may receive the outpouring of the Spirit:

> Not one of us will ever receive the seal of God while our characters have one spot or stain upon them. It is left with us to remedy the defects in our characters, to cleanse the soul temple

of every defilement. Then the latter rain will fall upon us as the early rain fell upon the disciples on the Day of Pentecost.[28]

Some of us may tend to recoil from strong statements such as this. But that response may be a signal that we need to evaluate our state and our standing with God.

Part Two of this book endeavors to deal with the matter of the cleansing of the soul and many related subjects. Meanwhile, let us remind ourselves of one text, a very familiar one: "If we confess our sins, He is faithful and just to forgive us our sins and to cleanse us from all unrighteousness" (1 John 1:9).

If we straightforwardly confess, trying to hide nothing, rationalize nothing, hold nothing back, He forgives, fully, unreservedly. And He cleanses us so that not "one spot or stain" is remaining upon our souls.

> Christ is able to save to the uttermost all who come to Him in faith. He will cleanse them from all defilement if they will let Him. But if they cling to their sins, they cannot possibly be saved; for Christ's righteousness covers no sin unrepented of.[29]

The Testing of the Father

Not only must Christians who receive the latter rain have been preparing daily for its reception; God will previously test every one who receives it to disclose whether each can be trusted with that Gift.

> Before giving us the baptism of the Holy Spirit, our heavenly Father will try us, to see if we can live without dishonoring Him.[30]

> The third angel's message is to lighten the earth with its glory; but only those who have withstood temptation in the strength of the Mighty One will be permitted to act a part in proclaiming it when it shall have swelled into the loud cry.[31]

Note, now, the assurance in these words:

> When a man is filled with the Holy Spirit, the more severely he is tested and tried, the more clearly he proves that he is a true representative of Christ in word, in spirit, in action.[32]

> Those who come up to every point, and stand every test, and overcome, be the price what it may, have heeded the counsel of the True Witness, and they will be fitted by the latter rain for translation.[33]

The servant of the Lord draws a parallel between Christ's transfiguration and the latter rain experience of His people. Jesus was spiritually ready for the ultimate test but, approaching the cross, He needed physical and moral strengthening and encouragement for the experience. He received it at the transfiguration. So God's people who are to go through the time of trouble and the plagues will be spiritually ready but will receive needed strength and encouragement for that ordeal from the latter rain.

> At the transfiguration, Jesus was glorified by His Father. . . . Thus before His betrayal and crucifixion He was strengthened for His last dreadful sufferings. As the members of the body of Christ approach the period of their last conflict, "the time of Jacob's trouble," they will grow up into Christ, and will partake largely of His spirit. . . . It is the latter rain which revives and strengthens them to pass through the time of trouble. Their faces will shine with the glory of that light which attends the third angel.[34]

The picture is clear. It is not the careless, the casual, the spiritually indolent, who receive the latter rain. It is not the unprepared who will receive it. It does not come upon the neglectful to awaken them and give them a power to overcome sin. The latter rain comes upon a prepared, victorious people to fit them to go out and finish the work, to make them ready for the great time of trouble, and to prepare them to meet Jesus face to face.

> The refreshing or power of God comes only on those who have prepared themselves for it.[35]

The Rain and the Harvest

A minister friend of mine began his ministry as pastor in one of the great wheat-growing provinces of Canada. Many of the church members were wheat farmers.

One late-summer day he was visiting one of those members, who invited him to go with him to take a look at the wheat. Together they walked into the golden grain, waist-tall all around them, acre upon rolling acre.

As they stood admiring the promising crop, the farmer plucked a few heads of wheat and rubbed them together in his hands, separating the grains from the chaff.

Examining the kernels with an expert eye he observed, "This wheat needs one more good rain to be ready for harvest."

> While we cherish the blessing of the early rain, we must not, on the other hand, lose sight of the fact that without the latter rain, to fill out the ears and ripen the grain, the harvest will not be ready for the sickle, and the labor of the sower will have been in vain.[36]

But had that farmer's grain been stubby, immature, it could have received no benefits from the final rain. No growth would have resulted from it. That which had been stunted would be stunted still.

The same situation will apply to God's professed people who have not been growing spiritually. They will be able to receive no benefits from the final outpouring of the Spirit.

> Are we looking forward to the latter rain, confidently hoping for a better day, when the church shall be endued with power from on high and thus fitted for work? The latter rain will never refresh and invigorate the indolent, who do not use the powers God has given them [today].[37]

How, Then, May We Be Ready?

How may we be ready for the latter rain? We have touched on some problems which show us what we must do to clear the way for it, and we have examined some positive steps that must be taken to be ready for it.

With these things clearly in mind, our answer can be summarized in one simple statement: "If you are right with God today, you are ready if Christ should come today."

In the context of the latter rain, we may paraphrase this statement thus: "If you are right with God today, you are ready if the latter rain should fall today."

The statement goes on to tell us what being right means:

> What we need is Christ formed within, the hope of glory.[38]

> We have now the invitations of mercy to become vessels unto honor, and then we need not worry about the latter rain; all we have to do is to keep the vessel clean and prepared and right side up, for the reception of the heavenly rain.[39]

Ellen White goes on to further qualify this statement: In order to receive that rain the vessel, the heart, must be thoroughly cleansed of all iniquity and defilement, and self must be crucified—now.

> It is our work today to yield our souls to Christ, that we may be fitted for the time of refreshing from the presence of the Lord— fitted for the baptism of the Holy Spirit.[40]

> It is the time of the latter rain, when the Lord will give largely of His Spirit.[41]

> Ask the Lord for rain in the time of the latter rain. The Lord . . . will give them showers of rain (Zechariah 10:1).

> For I will pour water on him who is thirsty, and floods on the dry ground (Isaiah 44:3).

[1] White, *The Acts of the Apostles,* pages 54, 55.
[2] White, *Testimonies to Ministers,* page 506.
[3] Ibid.
[4] Ibid., page 512.
[5] White, *The Great Controversy,* page 612.
[6] White, *Testimonies to Ministers,* page 509.
[7] White, *Maranatha,* page 61. See also *Testimonies for the Church,* Volume 5, page 714–715.
[8] White, *Selected Message,* Volume 1, page 175.
[9] White, *Manuscript Releases,* Volume 4, page 338.
[10] White, *The Great Controversy,* page 613.
[11] White, *Testimonies to Ministers,* page 506.
[12] White, *Counsels to Parents, Teachers, and Students,* page 532.
[13] White, *Testimonies to Ministers,* page 507.
[14] White, *Seventh-day Adventist Bible Commentary,* Volume 7, page 984.
[15] White, *Testimonies to Ministers,* page 399.
[16] White, *Christian Service,* page 228.
[17] White, *Early Writings,* page 71.
[18] White, *Testimonies for the Church,* Volume 1, page 261.
[19] White, *Maranatha,* page 212.
[20] White, *Seventh-day Adventist Bible Commentary,* Volume 4, page 1161.
[21] White, *Seventh-day Adventist Bible Commentary,* Volume 7, page 984.
[22] White, *Testimonies to Ministers,* page 399.
[23] White, *Review and Herald,* November 26, 1903.
[24] See *Daily Bulletin of the General Conference,* February 5, 1893, page 152.

[25] White, *Testimonies for the Church*, Volume 8, page 47.

[26] White, *Selected Messages*, Book 1, page 191.

[27] White, *Evangelism*, pages 697, 698.

[28] White, *Testimonies for the Church*, Volume 5, page 214.

[29] White, *Seventh-day Adventist Bible Commentary*, Volume 7, page 931.

[30] White, Letter 22, 1902.

[31] White, *Review and Herald*, November 19, 1908.

[32] White, *Manuscript Releases*, Volume 1, page 370.

[33] White, *Spiritual Gifts*, Volume 2, page 226.

[34] White, *Testimonies for the Church*, Volume 1, page 353.

[35] Ibid., page 619.

[36] White, *Testimonies to Ministers*, page 507, 508.

[37] White, *Maranatha*, page 212.

[38] White, *In Heavenly Places*, page 227.

[39] White, *Manuscript Releases*, Volume 1, page 179.

[40] White, *Evangelism*, page 702.

[41] White, *Testimonies to Ministers*, page 512.

PART TWO

Chapter 3
God's Part:
The Drawing of God

The people who receive the latter rain will have come to realize that, as members of the Laodicean church, there has been a closed door between themselves and the Savior which has hindered Him from entering their hearts and giving them an experience essential for salvation. Because of God's drawing, they began to understand they needed the former rain experience before they could be ready for the latter rain.

And I, if I be lifted up from the earth, will draw all men unto me (John 12:32, KJV).

Wartime England. Late 1944. As a medical orderly wearing the uniform of the Royal Canadian Air Force, I was attached to a small hospital on a Canadian bomber station in northern England.

Baptized a Seventh-day Adventist a half-dozen years previously, I had been attending an Adventist college before joining the Air Force. A year after joining I found myself in England.

For a time the thrill of being in storied England and, to a degree, connected with the great air armadas helping to end the war with Germany, took my attention. But in time the romance faded, the routine became dull, and boredom and discontent were my frequent companions.

Meanwhile, I had joined the ranks of the lukewarm Laodiceans. My Christian experience was at a low ebb, and my lifestyle poorly reflected Adventist standards.

I had been in this condition for some months when the Holy Spirit started to work upon me. Because of His constraint I began to be very moody, a state which continued for many weeks. One day I might be in the depths of gloom, and the next, in high spirits.

This became so pronounced that on one occasion my sergeant said to me, "You are the moodiest person I have met in all my life."

He, of course, could not have understood the reason for this. But I knew it was because the Holy Spirit was wooing, drawing me, and I was struggling under that constraint.

Drawn by the Moral Magnet

Heaven has ordained that the cross shall be the crux of the moral universe, the moral magnet toward which not only humanity, but the whole immense, intelligent creation is drawn.[1] Indeed, this little planet on which Jesus' cross was uplifted is destined, it would seem, ultimately to be the center of the universe (Revelation 21:1–3)—and all because of that cross.

All the saving power of the universe, then, is centered in, and flows from, the cross of Christ. Aside from the cross there is nothing.

> The only plan that could be devised to save the human race was that which called for the incarnation, humiliation, and crucifixion of the Son of God, the Majesty of heaven.[2]

The concept of drawing suggests undesirable distance between. It could also suggest resistance. This drawing is going on for the lukewarm Laodiceans. True, the metaphor of Revelation 3:14–22 does not explicitly contain the idea of drawing. But it does so implicitly. Let me illustrate.

George and his wife, Marge, have a disagreement which results in some words. After a time Marge flounces out of the living room, goes to the bedroom, and closes the door. That closed door is a symbol of the obstruction in their relationship.

Time passes. Then Marge hears a soft tapping at the door. At first she does not respond. But the knock comes again. That knocking finally softens her attitude, draws her to the door, induces her to open it, and, we would hope, contributes to their finding accord once more.

The closed door, and the continued knocking, of Revelation 3 speak of the Laodicean heart unsurrendered, self undenied.

The picture of Jesus knocking illustrates His endeavor to gain our attention and to draw us to Himself so that we will open our heart's door, and surrender ourselves to Him that He may become Lord of our hearts and everything in our lives.

It is the Nature of Love to Draw

What is it that draws us to Jesus? To the cross? There are many things, all of which are summarized by love, and issue from love.

Because God is love, He cannot help but love. And it is the nature of love to draw. Thus the Lord said of recalcitrant Israel, through Hosea, "I drew them with gentle cords, with bands of love" (Hosea 11:4).

His love for us, shown in so many ways, reaches forth, as rays reach out from the sun, to affect all it touches.

Christ's drawing love is moral, not irresistible. It is, someone has observed, "the divine response to man's inability."

God looked down at man in his lostness—and let us remember, that includes you and me—in his helplessness, his blindness, his appalling unawareness of his condition. And the divine love of Father and Son went out in sympathy inexpressible and a longing to help that we can never apprehend. And from that sympathetic longing, love reached out through the vast, cold, black remoteness sin had created between us and God, to touch and warm to spiritual life the unfeeling, sinful heart, unable of itself to respond. For, said Jesus, "no one can come to Me unless the Father . . . draws him" (John 6:44). "No one seeks God, but God seeks us all," a French Christian philosopher remarked. In the words of the hymn, God "loved me when I sought Him not."

And except the heart stubbornly remains as hard as a stone in the sun, it is attracted to turn as a flower to the warmth of that love, and to unfold and grow. That is what divine love, responded to, does to one.

(We might remark that one does not have to be an outright atheist or skeptic to be hard. One may sit in a church pew Sabbath after Sabbath and have that attitude.)

This stubborn unwillingness offers an answer to a question that sometimes comes to us.

Does Christ Really Draw All Men to Himself?

It seems obvious that all men are not so drawn. Does this prove Christ cannot really do what He said He would?

This objection was raised by a young man who had been invited by a minister to surrender his life to the Lord.

"Tell me," said the minister, "do you believe there is such a thing as gravitation?"

"Why, of course I do."

"Well, what is it?"

"It has been defined as the invisible force by which all matter on earth is drawn toward its center."

The preacher went to his study window and motioned for the young man to join him.

"You see those gilt balls, do you not?" he asked, pointing to the pawnbroker's symbol hanging outside a shop across the street.

"Yes."

"But what about the power of gravitation? You tell me that it is the force which pulls all matter toward the earth, yet those balls have been suspended there for years."

"Oh, well, they are fastened to that iron," the young man answered, his face reddening.

"Exactly," said the minister. "And so it is that men are not drawn to Christ, for they are bound by sins of one kind or another—ambition, business, pleasures, lusts. These are the things that hold men as with chains and keep them from surrendering to the constraining love of Christ."

God Loves that Which Needs Love

We observed that because the nature of God is love, He cannot but love. And it has been pointed out that it is not the attractiveness of the object of His love, but the character of that love itself, which accounts for its steadfastness. He loves that which needs love. Thus, difficult as it may be for us to understand sometimes, He loves the unlovable as much as the lovable. And as it is the nature of water to seek the lowest level, so it is the nature of God's love to flow to those who by their sinfulness need that love. As it is the nature of the sun to shine on all alike, so it is with God's love. "God shows no partiality" (Acts 10:34).

Our moral malformation, our peevish littleness, our rebelliousness, would have turned any lesser love away from the race millenniums ago. But we hear in the mournful question of God to His ancient people in their unrepentance, "How can I give you up, Ephraim?" (Hosea 11:8), an echo of His love for every one of us. And in the still more plaintive cry of Christ, "O Jerusalem, Jerusalem, the one who kills the prophets and stones those who are sent to her! How often I wanted to gather your children together, as a hen gathers her chicks under her wings, but you were not willing!" (Matthew 23:37), we hear the terrible heartbreak of Deity for His people of all ages who spurn heaven's love. And still the love of God flows on.

"Through all, His [God's] love is unchangeable. The waves of mercy may be beaten back, but again and again they flow to the hearts of undeserving human beings."[3] "Love never fails" (1 Corinthians 13:8). Love forever draws. Jesus' love saves the surrendered sinner from doom.

> God demonstrates His own love toward us, in that while we were still sinners, Christ died for us. Much more then, having now been justified by His blood, we shall be saved from wrath through Him (Romans 5:8, 9).

Only occasionally does the significance of this statement strike us in all its implications. Our imaginations cannot for long dwell on the horror of the final wrath, or for long retain the force of the subject. When the realization of this redemption from that doom does strike home, what gratitude fills the heart.

There are many who feel the drawing of Christ, not a few of whom attend church week after week, who realize their need, and experience a profound dissatisfaction with their spiritual condition, but have never been able to find anything to satisfy that need. The voice of conscience is ignored, or not understood, the drug of habit has dulled them to spiritual lethargy, the chains of sin bind them close so that they do not seem able to shake off their bonds.

But when people, warmed, respond and are melted, it is because they begin truly to appreciate the nature and magnitude of what the love and grace of God have done for them.

Is God's Love Just a "Warm Fuzzy"?

That God's love is more than a "warm fuzzy," is a fact not always appreciated. While "warm fuzzies" have their place, it seems to me they are inclined to appeal to that which is immature in us. We may look to them for comfort and perhaps security when our real needs are, from the human side, discomfort and insecurity. For, just as children can never learn to meet the real world and develop character by being overly sheltered by their parents, so God must sometimes show His love and make His appeals by the only means He knows will work under the circumstances. So, to win people, John Wesley wrote, "God uses all manner of ways; He tries every avenue of their souls. He applies sometimes to their understanding, showing them the folly of their sins; sometimes to their affections, tenderly expostulating

39

with them for their ingratitude, and even condescending to ask, 'What could I have done for you (consistent with my eternal purpose, not to force you) which I have not done?' He intermixes sometimes threats,—'Except ye repent, ye shall all likewise perish;' sometimes promises,— 'Your sins and your iniquities will I remember no more.' "[4]

Because of the love that reaches out in that drawing and makes the heart tender, there wells up within us a desire to experience the heart transformation of God's grace, a longing to know His compassionate mercy in our lives, a craving for forgiveness and cleansing, a wistfulness to have a conscience that no longer accuses. There is a wanting to feel clean, innocent, a desire to be freed from make-believe, a wistfulness to be the kind of people Christ wants us to be. There comes an eagerness to experience deliverance from the tyranny of self, a craving to conquer the curse of impatience, a wistfulness not simply to have to bank the fires of the volcano of anger, but to know that it no longer burns. There is a wanting to have mastery of the sins that so easily beset us. There is a seeking to know "the experimental knowledge of God and of Jesus Christ whom He has sent [that] transforms man into the image of God. It gives to man the mastery of himself, bringing every impulse and passion of the lower nature under the control of the higher powers of the mind."[5]

These longing impulses in the soul of Laodiceans is an indication that God is trying to alert them to their condition and needs, and to draw them to open their hearts to Himself.

Misunderstood Blessings

In trying to draw us to Himself God sometimes blesses us, and we take those blessings for approval. We take them as proof that we are right with Him, just as the Jews anciently believed that the fact that a man was rich was evidence God looked upon Him with approval. An experience we had years ago gave us a vivid illustration of this.

A young couple came to my wife and me for counsel. They had been Seventh-day Adventists for only a few months, and had joined the church because of what we agreed was a miracle. They had both been on hard drugs, and had become slaves of the habit. Eventually they became aware of their situation, and got scared of the grip the drugs had on them. They tried to kick the habit, but were helpless. Finally, in impotent desperation, they cried to God for deliverance. And their prayers were answered. They lost all desire for the drugs. Elated at what God had done, they joined the

Seventh-day Adventist Church. But, they confided to us, their marriage was like a thread tensioned across the sharp edge of a knife blade. They were "fighting like cats and dogs," and it would take very little for their marriage to be finished.

We tried as delicately and diplomatically as we knew how, to help them catch the idea that the problem, as it appeared to us, was that they had not really found a complete relationship with Jesus. He had delivered them from drugs to show them what He could do in every area of their lives if they would surrender totally to Him. We pointed out that if they would make that surrender, if, for example, each would give up to God the right to run the other's life or to expect the spouse to conform to his or her ideas, in His strength they would be able to resolve their difficulties and live together in peace.

But they rejected our suggestion that they needed a deeper commitment. To them, the fact that God had worked a miracle in their lives was proof positive they were accepted of Him and born again.

The experience of the Israelites during the wilderness wanderings proves this is not necessarily so. For forty years God fed them with manna, miraculously provided water for them, preserved their clothes and footwear from wearing out, and protected them in many ways. (See 1 Corinthians 10:1–4.) Yet "with most of them God was not well pleased" (verse 5). And there was a rabbinic saying that "the generation in the wilderness have no part in the life to come." Again, in the following passage we have the implication that one may move far toward God, and believe himself or herself to be a Christian. But this does not prove one is born again: "It is true that men sometimes become ashamed of their sinful ways, and give up some of their evil habits, before they are conscious that they are being drawn to Christ. But whenever they make an effort to reform, from a sincere desire to do right, it is the power of Christ that is drawing them."[6] But, we read in the next paragraph, "The sinner may resist this love, may refuse to be drawn to Christ; but if he does not resist he will be drawn to Jesus."

And when the sordid story of our world is done, God will be able to say to all—saved and lost alike, "I have drawn thee." And none will then be able to say, "Nay."

He Draws; Simply Come

There is nothing—nothing—we have to do to come to Jesus beyond simply responding to His drawing. Come. Simply allow Him to draw us.

We don't necessarily even have to feel sorry, really. Confession is not under discussion—at this point. Repentance is still a step or two ahead. We don't have to do those things at this stage because we can't, of ourselves. In our sinful natures we are inclined to be unwilling, and we are unable to come to Him. So sorrow for sins, and repentance, and all those things are, at this stage, His business, not ours.

I repeat again, we don't have to do anything, but simply allow Him to draw us to Himself. All we need to do is put ourselves into His hands, and be willing for Him to take us, step by step, along the route we need to go. When we do that—when we *really* do that—He will make us sorry for our sins as necessary. The Holy Spirit will give us repentance and will prompt us at the right time to confess our sins and to make them right with others as we may need to. *But we must be sure to take each step as He prompts us.*

"The Lord specifies no conditions except that you hunger for His mercy, desiring His counsel, and long for His love."[7]

God's words for lukewarm Laodiceans, His present-day, professed people, is the same as those He spoke with such pathos to Israel through Jeremiah more than two-and-a-half millenniums ago: "I have loved you with an everlasting love; therefore with lovingkindness I have drawn you" (Jeremiah 31:3).

God's lovingkindness is eternal, unchangeable, but for His earthly children His drawing cannot be eternal. The very nature of our fleeting existence precludes it. The proclivity of the human mind and character to set in unalterable patterns after so long, the tendency in time for human sensitivity to become callous to impulses unresponded to— each limits the feasibility and possibility of God drawing an individual after a period of time, known only to Himself.

"So be sure you do not refuse to hear the voice that speaks," Paul wrote to Jewish Christians almost two thousand years ago. "For if they who refused to hear those who spoke to them on earth did not escape, how little chance of escape is there for us if we refuse to hear the One who speaks from heaven" (Hebrews 12:25, Phillips).

1. The Greek of John 2:32 does not have "men," but simply "all." "Men" is indeed implied, and supplied. ("People" would be a better term.) But the biblical and Spirit of Prophecy picture is that much more is included than just humanity. See Col. 1:20; Ellen G. White on John 3:14–17, *Seventh-day Adventist Bible Commentary*, vol. 5, p. 1132.
2. White, Ellen G., *Signs of the Times*, January 20, 1890.
3. White, *Signs of the Times*, September 10, 1896.

4. Wesley, John, *Works,* Volume X, pages 233, 234, quoted in *A Theology of Love,* by Mildred Bangs Wynkoop, (Kansas City, MO: Beacon Hill Press of Kansas City, ©1972), page 88.
5. White, *Reflecting Christ,* page 117.
6. White, *Steps to Christ,* page 27.
7. White, *Selected Messages,* Volume 1, page 332.

Chapter 4
Our Part: Do Not Resist

T*he people who receive the latter rain will have learned to hear "the slightest whisper" of God to the conscience and will endeavor faithfully to respond to it.*

Two men faced each other across a table. One of them was speaking earnestly, entreatingly to the other as a solemnity rested upon all in the room.

When the speaker had finished his touching appeal, he extended his hand across the table and said to the other, his voice choking with emotion, "Come, Brother Jones, come!"

The second man arose and started to reach out his hand to clasp the other's. Then he hesitated and drew it back.

The other continued tearfully to plead with extended hand, "Come Brother Jones, come!"

Again the other began to reach across the table. Again he hesitated. Again he withdrew.

This happened several times. The last time the hands almost met. Then suddenly the second man pulled his hand back and sat down exclaiming, "No, no, never!"

And that incident of May 31, 1909, effectively ended any further significant relationship A. T. Jones had with the Seventh-day Adventist Church and its leaders.

What caused A. T. Jones to refuse to take General Conference President A. G. Daniells' hand in reconciliation with him and the church? We can never truly know, for we cannot know the thoughts and feelings of his heart. But we can reasonably conclude that pride was not the smallest factor involved. And, generally, the more visible the situation, the more prominent the individual, the harder it could be for him or her to "lose face." This was certainly one reason why the Pharisees could not back down and acknowledge Jesus as the Messiah. And, wrote Ellen White, "the spirit of Pharisaism is the spirit of human nature."[1]

It is hard for people who have thought they had a genuine experience with Jesus to be shown they are mistaken. Nicodemus, the rich, learned, and honorable Pharisee, a leader in the church, "was startled at the thought of a kingdom too pure for him to see in his present state. . . . He felt that he needed no change."[2] He was irritated by Jesus' suggestion that *he* needed a new birth. "The pride of the Pharisee was struggling against the honest desire of the seeker after truth."[3] So it may often be in people who may be similarly situated as was Nicodemus.

The following words of Ellen White come to mind. May they not have an application, both to Nicodemus, and to some of us?

> A faultless creed and a carnal life are too often found together in professed believers.[4]

This suggests a type of person who is difficult to reach. Like the Pharisees, they subscribe to all the "laws of Moses," and may feel secure in that belief. Their Christianity is intellectual, formal, but not of the heart. Thus there is a danger of being deceived by mistaking the semblance for the reality, of confusing rectitude of the outward life with inward righteousness.

"Many keep the truth in the outer court," to quote Ellen White again. "Its sacred principles have not a controlling influence over the words, the thoughts, the actions."[5]

How subtly then pride, conceit, self-seeking, power-seeking, rivalry, jealousy, envy, resentment, malice, avarice, and so many other covert sins can find a place in mind and heart, and inhibit the Holy Spirit's efforts to break through our Laodicean blindness. How easily small dishonesties, seemingly trivial deceits, can tarnish the soul, blur spiritual perception, and burden the conscience. The scary part is that this can happen so stealthily that one is hardly aware of what has taken place.

The Most Hopeless Sin

Resistance to God's drawings is probably almost always linked with pride. "Of all sins it [pride] is the most hopeless, the most incurable."[6] It closes the door against light and God.

It is hard for people who, like Nicodemus, thought they had a genuine experience with God to have it dawn on them that they were mistaken.

Every human heart knows the presence of pride, whether acknowledged or not. Pride, sensitive in the extreme, is ready to step from behind the curtain and take center stage at small provocation. A challenge to one's authority, an incursion on one's turf, a disputing of one's rights, a seeming questioning of one's judgment or opinion, a suggestion that one's long-held dogmas or opinions are wrong, a doubt raised about one's learning, an obstructing of one's ambitions, and instantly pride bestirs itself to protect, defend, push, rationalize, resist, or do whatever is necessary to safeguard the ego, or "save face" as Orientals have it. (Someone has described "ego" as an acronym for "Easing God Out.")

Some time ago I received an adult education brochure from a certain university which listed a course on pride. "Pride has a thousand faces," the introduction said. "Mountains out of Molehills; Always Making Excuses; Always the Last Word; Afraid to Make Mistakes; Stubbornness Looks Like Will Power; Inferiority Looks Like Superiority. There are very few books on pride and no civil laws against it. It is an attitude of mind and heart that distorts one's personality, ruins lives, poisons society, and topples civilizations."

A Battle with Pride

Vivid in my memory is a battle I had with pride on one occasion while working as an editor at the Review and Herald Publishing Association. A situation had developed in which I was tempted to feel I had been treated shabbily and not accorded a recognition I thought should have been mine. As I sat at my desk, I allowed myself to brood over the circumstance. Hurt pride gave birth to resentment, selfish ambition, envy, and other wrong feelings, all of which began to seethe together in my mind like an iniquitous witches' brew bubbling over a smoky fire in some foul and evil kitchen. And as I brooded, the fire got hotter and the pot seethed more fiercely.

After awhile I began to fight the thoughts and feelings, but self and pride were stronger than I. I could not put the matter from my mind.

Finally, unable to concentrate on my work, I left my office and went for a walk away from the building. As I walked, a battle was going on inside. I knew my attitude was wrong, sinful, destructive. I knew I could not resolve the matter within myself until I was willing to surrender my pride. But that was extremely hard to do. Didn't I have a right to feel as I did?

All the time I was praying for God to help me. But the decision had to be mine. Not until I was willing to turn the matter over to Him could He do much about it. And self dies hard.

At last, after walking and battling for perhaps a half hour, I thrust pride aside with a resolute effort of will, and surrendered the whole matter into God's hands.

Immediately the fire under the pot died down. The brew stopped seething. I knew a liberating peace. God had given me victory over pride and hurt feelings—when I was fully *willing* to give them up.

There is a small sequel to that experience. After pride had been attended to, and I could look at the whole thing rationally, I saw how small and unimportant it all was. Yet it forced me to "go to the mat" with myself.

But there was another thing, something that was not so small.

Sometimes the decision we make, the path we take on a small matter decides the ultimate orientation of our lives, and can make all the difference as to our eternal destiny. I do not know, but that occasion could have been just such a moment for me.

The Chief Sin

Pride has been called "the font of sin." It is not. The font of sin is self. The chief sin is selfishness. While pride may be first in the hierarchy of sins springing from selfishness, it, as well as all other sins, does originate in selfishness.

That which causes us to resist God's drawing, then, is self. And Jesus categorically stated "if anyone wants to follow in My footsteps, he must give up all right to himself, take up his cross and follow Me" (Matthew 16:24, Phillips).

Christ is here calling those who wish to become His followers to decisively choose to reject the imperious, demanding, self-devoted ego, to shoulder the cross (to be willing that self shall continually die) and day by day, moment by moment, to follow in the self-abnegating footsteps of His Master. He draws us to *His* cross, then He says, "Now, you take up *your* cross."

So we who would be wholly Christ's must do a very hard thing. We must give up all our rights. This requirement may be an exceedingly difficult one to swallow, but the Christian must come to see himself as having no rights, except as they are his in Christ. He says, "God, I am inclined to insist that I have some rights in this case, but You know best. So I place them in Your hands. Lead me to follow Your way in this situation, whatever it may be."

All our right to have our own way, to fulfill our own selfish desires; all our right to retaliate, to be resentful, to strive for the place or position we may actually have a right to, we must in faith turn over to God for His attention, believing He will do what is appropriate.

Moreover, we must give up the impulse to resist stubbornly when we know the other person is right. Because of self, resistance comes naturally to the fallen human race. It seems to be part of the equipment we are born with.

Some time ago I was listing to a pediatrician on a radio talk show. The topic was small children, and, by way of example, the pediatrician observed that little children will deliberately resist potty training—not for any buried, Freudian reason—but from just plain human contrariness, even at that tender age.

An experience I had at about age twelve comes to mind. It was Sabbath, and that morning I had heard a sermon which made a powerful impact on me. Today I can remember nothing of what was said. I cannot even recall who the preacher was. But I can still remember the effect of the sermon upon me.

I went home under the influence of that discourse, went to my room, and to my knees. I was under conviction that I needed to commit myself to God and confess whatever youthful sins I had in my life.

Looking back, I may have spent an hour there beside my bed, pleading with God to forgive and accept me. I can recall tears coursing down my cheeks as I pled for His approbation.

I Was Not Forgiven

Having read that, you may be at least surprised, and maybe shocked, when I write that I finally got up from my knees, knowing I was not forgiven and accepted.

"Do you really think God would not welcome you when you prayed and wept as you did?" a reader may ask in wonder.

"You did not have enough faith. That's why you felt you were not accepted," another will say.

It was not a matter of God welcoming me. It was not a matter of lack of faith. It was a matter of my not really surrendering myself to God. I suppose I was a bit like Esau. I wept tears of repentance, but at the same time, *in the back of my mind* I had reservations. I was willing to let go of a lot of boyish things. But I resisted letting *everything* go. I wanted to make some reservations, so that under some circumstances I could have my own way.

Really, you see, I still wanted to hang on to self. Some other things could go, but not self.

I fear that is the case with many of us Laodiceans. We want the latter rain. We want the blessings of God. But we are not quite willing to let self go so that we may have that experience. As was apparently the case with A. T. Jones, sometimes we are almost persuaded—but not quite.

The Christian psychiatrist, Paul Tournier, wrote that often "it is only the merest trifle that separates a person from the liberation he longs for—a paper partition." That may be so.

But that paper partition is often imposed by self and pride. And although God seeks to draw with the most poignant pleadings, although an individual may want God, that pride can sometimes make the partition as hard to demolish as if it were a meter thick and rock-solid.

A. W. Tozer illustrates this bizarre stubbornness: "You try to take a child's temperature or give him medicine or call a doctor and he will resist and howl. . . . In the next breath he will beg for help. 'Mama, I'm sick!' But he won't take a thing, he won't let you help him. . . .

"People will pray and ask God to be filled—but all the while there is that strange ingenuity, that contradiction within that prevents our wills from stirring to the point of letting God have His way."[7]

And when God's professed people are alive to self, so long as they stay that way, and are not willing to die to that self, as I, at twelve years of age, was not willing, God is not able to do much for them but seek to draw them and hope they will eventually get to the place where they will die.

Ellen White knew about people who were not dead. Writing to one brother, she commented, "Self is all alive, and you stand guard continually to preserve it from mortification [death] or insult. . . . You are not dead."[8]

So it is then, when we have died to self and sin, that God can revive us to spiritual life. And not before.

Parasol and All

The year was 1840. In March, William Miller held a series of meetings in a church in Portland, Maine, where thirteen-year-old Ellen Harmon, later Ellen White, lived. She attended Mr. Miller's meetings.

These meetings attracted great attention, and resulted in much heart searching, and praying, and confession of sins. In *Life Sketches* Mrs. White describes an incident that took place at one of the meetings.

My attention was attracted to a little girl who seemed to be in great distress. Her face would pale and flush by turns, as though she were passing through a severe conflict.

Tightly clasped in her arms was a pretty little parasol. Occasionally she would loosen her hold on it for a moment as if about to let it fall, then her grasp would tighten upon it again; all the time she seemed to be regarding it with a peculiar fascination. At last she cried out: "Dear Jesus, I want to love thee and go to heaven! Take away my sins! I give myself to thee, parasol and all." She threw herself into her mother's arms weeping and exclaiming: "Ma, I am so happy, for Jesus loves me, and I love him better than my parasol or anything else!"

The face of the child was fairly radiant, she had surrendered her little all. In her childish experience she had fought the battle and won the victory. There was much weeping and rejoicing in the tent. The mother was deeply moved and very joyful that the Lord had added her dear child as a lamb to his fold. She explained to those present that her little daughter had received the parasol as a present not long before. She was very much delighted with it, and had kept it in her hands most of the time, even taking it to bed with her.

During the meeting her tender heart had been moved to seek the Saviour. She had heard that nothing must be withheld from Jesus; that nothing short of an entire surrender of ourselves and all we have would be acceptable with him. The little parasol was the child's earthly treasure upon which her heart was set, and, in the struggle to give it up to the Lord, she had passed through a trial keener perhaps than that of the mature Christian, who sacrifices this world's treasures for the sake of Christ.
. . .

Many times in after life that little incident had been brought to my mind. When I saw men and women holding desperately to the riches and vanity of earth, yet anxiously praying for the love of Christ, I would think: 'How hard it is to give up the parasol!'[9]

William Barclay was quite correct when he said, "In the last analysis, the one thing which defeats God is the defiance of the human heart."[10]

"Why is it," Ellen White asks, "that we see so many clouded, mixed experiences? . . . It is because they [the people in that condition] have not responded to the drawing of Christ."[11]

A Question for Myself and You

May I pose a question? It's one for myself, and for you. While I may ostensibly have made every sacrifice for God, am I, in my secret heart hanging onto self and so resisting God, and thus maintaining in my heart a barrier which makes it virtually impossible for God to accomplish even the work of the former rain in me?

Constantly we need to pray, "Lord, if I am in any respect hanging onto self, help me to be willing to be made willing to make a complete and unconditional submission to You."

> The Father sets His love upon His elect people who live in the midst of men. These are the people whom Christ has redeemed by the price of His own blood; and because they respond to the drawing of Christ, through the sovereign mercy of God, they are elected to be saved as His obedient children. Upon them is manifested the free grace of God, the love wherewith He hath loved them. Everyone who will humble himself as a little child, who will receive and obey the word of God with a child's simplicity, will be among the elect of God.[12]

To repeat what we observed at the end of the previous chapter: Primarily, at this stage *God wants only one thing of us*—that we submit to Him. When we do that He will lead us along the next step in our experience.

1. White, Ellen G., *Thoughts from the Mount of Blessing*, page 79.
2. White, *The Desire of Ages*, page 171.
3. Ibid.
4. White, *Review and Herald*, October 1, 1901.
5. Ibid.
6. White, *Christ's Object Lessons*, page 154.
7. Tozer, A. W., *I Talk Back to the Devil*, page 84.
8. White, *Testimonies for the Church*, Volume 2, page 425.
9. White, *Life Sketches*, pages 141, 142.
10. Barclay, William, *The Gospel of John*, (Edinburgh: The Saint Andrew Press, ©1963), page 223.
11. White, *Signs of the Times*, February 15, 1892.
12. White, *Our High Calling*, page 77.

Chapter 5
God's Part:
He Will Convict

Those of the once lukewarm Laodiceans who eventually receive the latter rain will have been convicted of their spiritual bankruptcy, and will be regenerated and transformed through the early rain without which experience they cannot possibly receive that final spiritual outpouring.

The first step in reconciliation to God is the conviction of sin.[1]

> As we yield to the influence of the Spirit of God, our conscience becomes tender and sensitive, and sin that we have passed by with little thought, becomes exceeding sinful.[2]

> It is through the influence of the Holy Spirit that we are convicted of sin, and feel our need of pardon. None but the contrite are forgiven; but it is the grace of God that makes the heart penitent. He is acquainted with all our weaknesses and infirmities, and He will help us.[3]

So we can thank God that He graciously convicts us of our sins. Did He not, we would never feel any need. As one old Bible teacher remarked: "In review of God's manifold blessings, the thing I seem most to thank Him for is the conviction of sin."

A Baffling Situation

As we think about that conviction, we are, once again, confronted with the baffling state in which God finds the Laodiceans. It is like a problem situation in which the person involved does not see that there is a problem, and indeed insists there is none.

C. S. Lewis highlights the Laodicean situation when he points out that you know you've been asleep when you are awake, not when you are sleeping. The Laodicean description suggests we are spiritually asleep, and have the unawareness of the sleeper.

There are those who would assure the Laodiceans they do not need to feel guilty, which is an element in conviction of sin. The secular psychologist might suggest that guilt is merely a neurotic symptom (which, in some cases, it indeed may be), "not a matter for expiation but for explanation," in the words of William K. Kilpatrick. Others, some of whom are preachers, would say that feelings of guilt are simply the devil trying to make you feel bad, and that God does not do that. For one to say or do anything to cause another person to feel guilty, they insist, is to bring discouragement, and it is wrong to discourage anybody.

I am reminded of a comment by Samuel Koranteng-Pipim, in which he points out the current philosophy that a situation causing suffering to the individual is to be avoided. "The 'trickle down' effect of this pleasure-pain principle on Christian lifestyle is the belief shared by many Christians that a believer cannot and must not suffer pain—a philosophy that runs contrary to the biblical teaching that sometimes obedience to Christ may involve suffering (1 Peter 2:20; 3:13–17; 2 Timothy 3:12; Revelation 2:10)."[4]

There are times when, confronted with our sinful state and our sins, we may indeed become discouraged. Assuredly, God does not deliberately give occasion for discouragement. But He sometimes permits it, just as, in love and pity, He permits other undesirable experiences to come to us, knowing that there are blessings to be extracted from them, if we respond to them correctly. So the soul fully convinced of its sinfulness is often tempted to despondency and to believe that it cannot be accepted by God. But let that soul remember that Christ died for his sins, and that now Jesus is our Substitute, a risen, living, justifying Savior.

Satan is keenly interested in what God is trying to do for us. If he sees we are under conviction of sin he may try to push us over the edge into discouragement or depression. His goal is to plunge us into the abyss of hopelessness.

But for one to urge that a sense of guilt is simply Satan trying to have his way, and that God has nothing to do with guilt, is incorrect, even dangerous.

To urge one to avoid doing or saying anything that might cause another person to feel guilty just because it could lead to discouragement is almost like urging a doctor not to prescribe some medication for someone with a particular disease because it might make him feel nauseated.

The eminent Swiss physician/psychiatrist Paul Tournier insists it is not guilt that is an obstacle to grace. Rather, "it is the repression of guilt, self-justification, genuine self-righteousness and smugness which is the obstacle."[5]

Temporary Discouragement or Eternal Death?

Yes, when our sinfulness is brought home to us we may, for the time, feel discouraged because of our sins, just as other things in life may occasionally tend to dishearten us. But is it better for one to feel some discouragement over his or her sins, or to die in those sins? And is not Jesus the remedy for sin and for the melancholy that may come as a result of conviction of sin?

I do not find that God avoids laying conviction of sin upon people because they might become discouraged. Nor do I find anything in Scripture that tells us we should avoid saying or doing anything that might lay conviction upon any person for fear he or she might become discouraged.

"When He [the Holy Spirit] has come, He will convict the world of sin [demonstrate, prove guiltiness] and of righteousness, and of judgment" (John 16:8). When Peter preached at Pentecost, he spoke so directly that his hearers were "cut to the heart" (Acts 2:37); Paul kicked against the pricks of a guilty conscience lain upon him by God (Acts 9:5, KJV).

> God does not send messengers to flatter the sinner. He delivers no message of peace to lull the unsanctified into fatal security. He lays heavy burdens upon the conscience of the wrongdoer, and pierces the soul with arrows of conviction. The ministering angels present to him the fearful judgments of God to deepen the sense of need, and prompt the cry, "What must I do to be saved?"[6]

Let's face it: a real conviction of sin brings suffering. In the words of James H. McConkey, we sometimes "come . . . into a place of struggle, of soul-agony; a consciousness of fierce resistance and of keenest suffering; of turmoil, uncertainty, and distress . . . a seemingly utter spiritual void, and barrenness in our souls."[7]

So true guilt comes from the things for which men are reproved by God within their innermost souls.

While we quote John 16:8 to prove that the Holy Spirit brings conviction of sin to an individual, we must continue beyond the first part of the text. For, as the *Beacon Dictionary of Theology* points out, "there is an accompanying offer of divine forgiveness and salvation. Thus [the text] combines *uncompromising* condemnation with a gracious call to repentance and an offer of salvation to those who repent. The many divine invitations to repentance and salvation found throughout the Bible make it clear that God's purpose for conviction is pardon, release, restoration."[8] [Emphasis in original.]

In what we refer to as the Laodicean condition we may believe all the right things and, so far as appearances are concerned, do all the right things, and on that basis gloss over or palliate our condition. As noted in the previous chapter, "A faultless creed and a carnal life are too often found together in professed believers."[9] (The term *carnal*, may connote gross sinfulness for some people. But it need mean nothing more than simply living primarily for self.) Man tends to be very indulgent to himself in this respect. And so we are inclined to have a lack of conviction of the sins and the sinfulness, which the True Witness clearly points out, are ours, and which we must therefore acknowledge. These conditions are often overlaid, buried under a layer of blasé heedlessness, while the conscience is half asleep. So we feel no acute need of repentance. True, occasionally there may be a vague sense of imperfection, a general conviction of lostness; but such shallow conviction will not be reformative unless it leads to a deeper persuasion of sin.

A Longing to Be Cleansed

When conviction truly lays hold upon the mind and heart "the sinner has a sense of the righteousness of Jehovah and feels the terror of appearing, in his own guilt and uncleanness, before the Searcher of hearts. He sees the love of God, the beauty of holiness, the joy of purity; he longs to be cleansed and to be restored to communion with Heaven."[10]

What must the majority of Laodiceans recognize in themselves to lead them to conviction?

Prefacing our answer to this question, we observe that it is the "Faithful and True Witness" who points out those conditions (Revelation 3:14). "The testimony, so cutting and severe, cannot be a mistake, for it is the True Witness who speaks, and His testimony must be correct."[11]

If we believe the True Witness also speaks through the Spirit of Prophecy, then we will accept that its witness is also correct, and is to be taken seriously.

The Spirit of Prophecy has a great deal to say in its amplification of Revelation's message to the Laodiceans. We saw some of it in chapter one. As we read the many pages in which Ellen White speaks to that church, we can sense her profound concern, and her struggle to express that concern in her writings so that you and I might understand the significance, seriousness, and urgency of her message. Sometimes she mentions her feelings of inadequacy, of her inability to write so as to stab home sufficiently to her readers the profound and eternal import of what she is trying to convey.

People truly serious about being prepared to receive the latter rain will not pass by what she says just because it may be disturbing, or take it for granted that the descriptions do not apply to them personally. They will not regard these matters as of little consequence for themselves, but will earnestly try to look at them squarely, honestly and prayerfully, and will endeavor to weigh them impartially to discover if, indeed, there is a personal application to be made.

Ellen White writes of many Laodiceans as "living in a spiritual self-deception,"[12] apparently seeing themselves as devout Christians. It may be observed that Christ's denunciations seem largely to have been directed toward the kind of people who appeared, and believed themselves to be, comparatively virtuous.

Here, then, is a very frightening condition in which one's religion may be on a very proper moral and ethical level. One may be living a respectable, useful life, and so may harbor the belief he is being saved from sin, while the real problem—the total unacceptability to God of the natural, sinful, human heart, whether "good" or bad—is not truly grasped.

Carl F. H. Henry notes that even pagans can live "good" lives. He quotes one writer as saying, "the ethical virtues of the Greeks . . . [were] nothing but natural impulses educated and disciplined by reason . . . the more dangerous because they [seemed] good."[13]

Internal Virtue, not Outward Conformity, Required

Without exception, the heart of every single human being must be changed; a new, spiritual heart must be transplanted into every one of us, before we are children of God. One does not become a Christian merely by changing his religious opinions or the outward aspects of his life, even though the changes may be radical. One does not become a Christian by living a commendable moral life, but by having a radical change of heart. As Carl Henry further notes, "Many religions [and religious people] are more concerned about outward conformity than about internal virtue."[14]

We perhaps need to note that "heart" refers to the moral core of the individual, which involves the thoughts, emotions, affections, attitudes, ambitions, desires, intentions, motives, will—the whole subjective inner life. And "the vileness of the [unregenerate] human heart is not understood."[15] (The "new heart" includes "the mind, the life, the whole being. . . . There is a daily, hourly dying to selfishness and pride.")[16]

Lukewarm Laodiceans must have a conviction of their need of the gold, the white raiment, and the eyesalve. "The gold tried in the fire is faith that works by love."[17] "The white raiment is the righteousness of Christ that may be *wrought* into the character."[18] The eyesalve, the Word of God which, applied to the eye, or conscience, makes it sensitive to its needs.[19] [Italics supplied.]

The faithful application of the Word, which opens the "eyes of the heart" of the lukewarm Christian and makes the conscience smart, will cause him to see that he is clothed in filthy spiritual rags. But how many people studiously, seriously, and habitually peruse the pages of the Word to find and supply their own spiritual needs?

The Laodiceans are described as feeling they have "need of nothing." One only needs this attitude to be a sinner—a lost sinner.

What Do I Need?

Another thing: I may say to myself, "I am a member of the Laodicean church, the majority of which is characterized as lukewarm. If I believe the Bible and Spirit of Prophecy, I must accept this evaluation. I probably don't have the kind of Christian experience I should have. But *what am I in need of?* So far as I can see, I'm as much a Christian as anyone else in the church."

Is it really possible for a church to be in the condition in which Laodiceans are described as being, without being aware of it?

The disturbing fact seems to be that Laodicea is mentally and, to a large degree, morally blind, and that only God can remove the scales from its eyes.

In this chapter we are looking at conviction. It may be said that conviction will accompany the drawing we discussed in chapter three. That is possible. It may. But for many people the loving drawing of Jesus and the Holy Spirit will be the factor that will be prominent in their consciousness at the time. As they submit to Jesus and are drawn closer to Him they will begin to see their sinfulness in contrast to His holiness. "The closer you come to Jesus, the more faulty you will appear in your own eyes."[20]

In chapter three we referred to Christ's drawing of the Laodiceans being shown by His knocking at the heart's door. When the door is opened, and the Savior invited in, the light of His presence illuminates the heart. Then, just as sunlight flooding into a room shows the dust floating in the air, so the light of Jesus shining in the life shows us the sin, and leads us to conviction

When God convicts us of sin, He does not contradict our consciences, but appeals to them. As He applies His Word to our hearts and memories, our consciences stand beside us to witness for or against us respecting how we have obeyed the law. It is thus, and only thus, that the Spirit can awaken us to our needs.

> In one way only can a true knowledge of self be obtained. We must behold Christ. It is ignorance of Him that makes men so uplifted in their own righteousness. When we contemplate His purity and excellence, we shall see our own weakness and poverty and defects as they really are. We shall see ourselves lost and hopeless, clad in garments of self-righteousness, like every other sinner. We shall see that if we are ever saved, it will not be through our own goodness, but through God's infinite grace.[21]

1. White, Ellen G., *The Great Controversy*, page 467.
2. White, *Our High Calling*, page 153.
3. White, *Selected Messages*, Book 1, page 353.
4. Koranteng-Pipim, Samuel, "Contemporary Culture and Christian Lifestyle: A Clash of Worldviews," *Journal of the Adventist Theological Society*, Volume 4, Number 1, Spring, 1993, page 140.
5. Tournier, Paul, *Guilt and Grace*, (New York: Harper and Row, ©1962), page 136.
6. White, *The Desire of Ages*, page 104.
7. McConkey, James H., *The Three-fold Secret of the Holy Spirit*, (Chicago: Moody Press, ©1897), pages 77, 78.
8. Taylor, Richard S., Editor, *Beacon Dictionary of Theology*, (Kansas City, MO: Beacon Hill Press of Kansas City, ©1983), page 136.
9. White, *Review and Herald*, October 1, 1901.
10. White, *Steps to Christ*, page 24.
11. White, *Testimonies for the Church*, Volume 3, page 253.
12. White, *Seventh-day Adventist Bible Commentary*, Volume 7, page 962.
13. Henry, Carl F. H., *Christian Personal Ethics*, (Grand Rapids: William B. Eerdmans Publishing Company, ©1957), page 457.

14. Ibid., page 192.
15. White, *Medical Ministry,* page 143.
16. White, *Sons and Daughters of God,* page 100.
17. White, *Christ's Object Lessons,* page 158.
18. White, *Seventh-day Adventist Bible Commentary,* Volume 7, page 965.
19. Ibid.
20. White, *Steps to Christ,* page 64.
21. White, *Christ's Object Lessons,* page 159.

Chapter 6
Our Part: Only Acknowledge that You Sinned

People who receive the latter rain, many of them once among the lukewarm, will have seen and frankly acknowledged the truth of Jesus' description of themselves as wretched, miserable, poor, blind, naked—and that in that condition they could not be saved. Having acknowledged their state, they have taken a crucial step which makes cleansing, or regeneration, possible, which is, of course, not possible until we accept the need of cleansing. Without cleansing, which is obviously an imperative for the reception of the former rain, no person can be ready for the latter rain.

After God convicts us of sin, He can do little more for us until we acknowledge our condition and needs. But acknowledgment of our sins must be preceded by our acceptance of God's evaluation of our sins and sinfulness. And this acceptance means more than merely mentally agreeing to a conviction that we have sinned. If it were no more than this, acceptance would be a simple thing. But embracing God's assessment of our sins means the recognition of moral and ethical demands that impinge upon every facet of our lives. Which would seem to account for the response of the atheist in the following story.

An atheist and a Christian got involved in a discussion of the resurrection of Christ, the atheist asserting that it was an impossibility. As they talked he brought up argument after argument why the doctrine of the resurrection was unacceptable. But the Christian demolished them, one by one, until he had none left.

At last the atheist burst out, "I admit you have proved the resurrection did take place. But I still do not believe in it, and I never will."

Incredible? Not really. For while this circumstance may be particularly glaring, the attitude is not as uncommon as we may think. Many an uncompromisingly defended personal theology is founded, not on biblical evidence, but on a position which offers less difficulty to the carnal human heart or human pride, or which permits one to protect or justify some weakness in the character, or allows for the promotion of a special credo.

So we would venture that the atheist rejected the resurrection, not on the basis that it was impossible. He admitted the evidence sustained it. He rejected it because he understood the moral claims it would make on him to concede it. And he was unwilling to accept them.

Accepting God's Evaluation of Our Sins

So, from the very first step on the Christian way, there must be a willingness to accept God's estimate of our sins, and to submit in faith to divine authority. This is because we are not in a position to define sin, or even to truly recognize it. Only God can truly define what it is. And God's evaluation of sin has not diminished or changed through the ages. "We should not try to lessen our guilt by excusing sin. We must accept God's estimate of sin, and that is heavy indeed."[1]

Nor dare we define right and wrong in terms of what the majority accepts, even among Seventh-day Adventists. History attests, time and time again, that the majority is often wrong, even in the church.

As a whole, twentieth century society denies or ignores the fact of sin. "Our society," wrote Arthur C. Custance, "is probably less concerned with sin than any society in history."[2] There is an easygoing attitude toward it. Yet one of the Christian's vital defenses against sin is the capacity to be shocked by it. As William Barclay said, "When we cease to take a serious view of sin we are in a perilous position."[3]

So I must accept God's evaluation of my sin and acknowledge that what He convicts me of is, indeed, the kind of sinner I am. "Only acknowledge your iniquity, that you have transgressed against the Lord your God," Jeremiah pleads (Jeremiah 3:13). Like the prodigal son we can only admit, "Father, I have sinned." At this stage this is all that we can do, this is all that is required—merely to admit to God, without reserve, that we are indeed sinners, that we have sinned, that we are indeed guilty of all He convicts us of. (And, incidentally, it is hard to admit you are a "prodigal" when, like the older brother, all the time you thought you were at home.)

There are times when conviction may be intellectual only. We are led to see, on the evidence of God's word, that we are sinners. The heart, however, may not be deeply convicted.

Ellen White writes of King Saul being in this condition. Commenting on his reaction to the prophet Samuel's condemnation of his self-justification at having sacrificed to God against instructions, she observes that because Saul acknowledged Samuel as a prophet of God, "he should have accepted the reproof, though he could not himself see that he had sinned."[4]

If, on the basis that God points it out in His Word, we acknowledge our sinfulness, even though we may have no emotional conviction, we make it possible for God to do a further work for us, and to lead us to a heart recognition and acknowledgement.

The Desire of Ages portrays the enormity of sin in its powerful and moving description of the final scenes of Christ's crucifixion:

> It was not the dread of death that weighed upon Him. It was not the pain and ignominy of the cross that caused His inexpressible agony. Christ was the prince of sufferers; but His suffering was from a sense of the malignity of sin, a knowledge that through familiarity with evil, man had become blinded to its enormity. Christ saw how deep is the hold of sin upon the human heart, how few would be willing to break from its power. He knew that without help from God, humanity must perish, and He saw multitudes perishing within reach of abundant help.[5]

So sin is a repulsive moral disease so virulently infectious that, in its effects, it has malevolently metastasized throughout all of nature. Humanity is corrupted by that disease. And you and I are one with humanity. As we read in *Education,* page 29, "The result of the eating of the tree of knowledge of good and evil is manifest in every man's experience. There is in his nature a bent to evil, a force which, unaided, he cannot resist."

You and I must, then, accept and acknowledge that we are naturally selfish. I must acknowledge, Yes, I am by nature a self-seeking, self-elevating, self-indulgent creature. Pride makes me quick to defend self, and sensitive to reproach or anything that would seem to attack my ego. I have to be right, so I sometimes stubbornly go to great lengths to prove my point, and so safeguard my vanity. And even when I know I am wrong, I often am tempted to not back down. Sometimes I give in to the temptation, at least for awhile.

Moreover, I am naturally tempted to gravitate to people or situations that will give me the greatest personal advantage or status. My human nature is prone to pull others down if that will contribute to elevating me. And I did not need to be taught these attitudes, only to refine them. They came with the model.

The Difficulty of Writing "I"

Writing the foregoing words was a somewhat uncomfortable experience for me. The personal pronoun "I" caused me some unease. It seems so revealing. I felt a little bit like Adam and Eve must have felt, standing naked before the Creator. It would have been much easier to hide behind the amorphous "we" and "us." That way, I would really be exposing nothing, or very little, of a personal nature: *We* are self-seeking, self-indulgent. Pride makes *us* quick to defend self. When *we* know we are wrong, *we* often will not back down.

Perhaps, reader, you experienced a bit of discomfort also, if while reading "I," you felt a personal application. If so, this tells us a bit about the nature of sin, doesn't it?

(At this place I need to tell you that I have surrendered my life to my Savior, and He gives me victory over my sinfulness as I depend continuously on Him. But I am reminded of Paul who "was in such constant dread, lest his evil propensities should get the better of him, that he was constantly battling, with firm resistance, unruly appetites and passions."[6] I am aware that in my flesh dwells nothing good and that it always tends to selfishness, so that in Christ I must constantly put to death the temptations of the flesh.)

So totally, unreservedly admitting to God that I am, by way of illustration, a potential liar, or a cheat, a pervert, a thief, a hypocrite, a glutton, or an angry person, envious, self-willed, deceitful, covetous, ambitious, avaricious, totally selfish, a murderer, or an adulterer; may take a great deal of grace, and an exertion of will that requires more strength than we ourselves have.

And, like David, one may be convicted for a long time before he becomes willing to accept his guilt and confess. Blinded and deceived by his exalted position, perhaps deluded by the philosophy that, as king, he could do no wrong, David had for a year refused to acknowledge that he had sinned. But even in that frame of mind he could not escape from the mental conflict that grew out of his base crime of adultery with Bathsheba and the murder of her husband. Thus he wrote, in his penitential prayer: "When I kept silent, my bones grew old through my groaning all the day long. For day and night Your hand was heavy upon me" (Psalm 32:3, 4).

Laodicea and the Modern Attitude Toward Sin

Laodicea has not escaped being affected by the modern attitude toward sin. This is one reason why liberal practices and perspectives have invaded our churches, schools, and other Seventh-day Adventist institutions. There is a steady process of secularization going on among us, one phase leading to another. It is a case of sin growing on what it feeds upon.

At the same time sin has been diluted in the thinking of many of us so that things that were once seen as wrong no longer appear so terrible.

Furthermore, even those who have surrendered to Jesus must be alert that their present perception of sin not be colored, and weakened by their past. For example, if in the past one who is now a Christian has viewed a lot of Hollywood movies with their explicit portrayals of sin, it may be that this familiarity will influence his attitude so that he may not immediately see as sinful, scenes that a more sensitive person will see as spiritually demoralizing.

There are other types of sins referred to in the Bible that are almost totally disregarded today. As reprehensible to God as outward deeds and actions, are sins of the mind (Mark 7:21)—or more so. There is the sin of anger. Put away, writes Paul, wrath—a sudden, boiling over of the feelings—and anger—a more settled state or condition of mind (Ephesians 4:31; Colossians 3:8).

Andrew Murray holds that one's tendency to exhibit anger or irritability is proof of whether Christ's love is in the heart or not.[7] The *Tyndale New Testament Commentaries* state that bad temper and unjustified anger, is a mark of the old nature.[8] (On the matter of justified anger, the commentary goes on to say that there is such a thing [Ephesians 4:26], but "the Christian must be sure that his anger is that of righteous indignation, and not just an expression of personal provocation or wounded pride. It must have no sinful motives, and not be allowed to lead us into sin in any way."[9]

And note this quotation:

> The law of God takes note of the jealousy, envy, hatred, malignity, revenge, lust, and ambition that surge through the soul, but have not found expression in outward action, because the

opportunity, not the will, has been wanting. And these sinful emotions will be brought into the account in the day when "God shall bring every work into judgment, with every secret thing, whether it be good, or whether it be evil" (Ecclesiastes. 12:14).[10]

Jesus made it plain that sins such as anger and lust are culpable in the eyes of God (Matthew 5:19–48).

When God takes the initiative and convicts of sin, the next step is ours: we must accept His decision as brought home to our minds by His Word and our consciences by His Spirit, and acknowledge that we have sinned, that we are sinners. Until we do, we make it impossible for God to take His next step—give us repentance. And without repentance, there can be no forgiveness and cleansing. God has to prepare us for this step. He leads us to the place where we can objectively look at ourselves. He brings us to the place where we are spiritually awake enough to see our condition.

When, before God, we have met squarely the fact that we are sinners and admitted it, He can infuse a sense of remorse for our sins, which is the attitude that makes it possible for us to confess, and without which we cannot genuinely confess.

The conviction of sin is sometimes easy to destroy. Indecision, simply doing nothing, will destroy it. In time, conviction shrivels and dies if not followed by action. And, like flowers in a vase, it may wilt quickly. A decision must be made soon.

One may, like Lucifer, choose not to see himself as wrong. Then, in blind self-confidence, he will find any number of reasons to "prove" he is not wrong, and no amount of evidence will change his mind and cause him to acknowledge he is wrong.

A full, candid acknowledgment of sin, admitting that we are wrong before God and toward our fellowmen, and that we are spiritually malformed, selfish, self-seeking beings, can be a harrowing, humiliating, pride-wrenching exercise, and thus many shrink back from it. Saul could never do it.

1. White, Ellen G., *Thoughts from the Mount of Blessing,* page 116.
2. Custance, Arthur C., *Man in Adam and in Christ,* (Grand Rapids: Zondervan Publishing House, ©1975), page 275.
3. Barclay, William, *The Letter to the Corinthians,* (Edinburgh: The Saint Andrew Press, ©1956), page 49.
4. White, *Patriarchs and Prophets,* page 633.

5. White, *The Desire of Ages,* page 752, 753.
6. White, *This Day With God,* page 277.
7. Murray, Andrew, *Absolute Surrender,* (Chicago: Moody Press, n.d.), page 29.
8. Tasker, R. V. G., Editor, "The Epistle of Paul to the Ephesians," *The Tyndale New Testament Commentaries,* (Grand Rapids: William B. Eerdmans Publishing Company, ©1981), page 133.
9. Ibid.
10. White, *Selected Messages,* Book 1, page 217.

Chapter 7
God's Part: Repentance, the Gift of God

P eople who will receive the latter rain will not only acknowledge their *sins after they are convicted of them, but will demonstrate the depth and genuineness of that acknowledgement by deep-down repentance which makes possible the prior work of the essential, former rain in their lives.*

Repentance is my looking back on my life and into my heart, and seeing myself for what I have been and am in the pure light that shines from the Savior and from the Moral Law. I am brought to remorse so that I reject my sinfulness, turn from sinful things and resolutely decide to follow God's ways now and in my future.

This decision is made because God has succeeded in causing me to perceive my life and myself a little like He sees them, and I have accepted that revelation. I glimpse something of the magnitude of my selfishness. I see a little of God's abhorrence of my sins. I sense His righteous condemnation, not of me, but of my transgressions. I agree with His evaluation of me and of my life. I experience heart sorrow for what I have done that is not in accord with His holiness, and I truly want no more to be that kind of person, just as He wants me no more to be that kind of person.

"I saw the humility of Jesus, and my pride;" said one Christian, "the meekness of Jesus, and my temper; the lowliness of Jesus, and my ambition; the purity of Jesus, and my unclean heart; the faithfulness of Jesus, and the deceitfulness of my heart; the unselfishness of Jesus, and my selfishness; the trust and faith of Jesus, and my doubts and unbelief; the holiness of Jesus, and my unholiness; and I came to loathe myself."[1]

Of the repentance of the Corinthians Paul wrote, "See what God did with this sadness of yours: how earnest it has made you, how eager to prove your innocence! Such indignation, such alarm, such feelings, such devotion" (2 Corinthians 7:11, TEV).

Everybody Must Repent

Acknowledging our sinfulness allows the redemptive waters to flow more freely, but this does not necessarily connote remorse. A child confronted with some misdemeanor may acknowledge that he has done it, but the attitude that goes with genuine confession may be missing.

Repentance is an imperative for all who will be saved. God cannot forgive until we repent (Acts 2:38). "Sins not repented of are sins not forgiven."[2] Yet repentance is frequently played down or neglected altogether in preparing people for church membership. "Many have accepted the theory of the truth who have had no true conversion. I know whereof I speak. There are few who feel true sorrow for sin, who have deep, pungent convictions of the depravity of the unregenerate nature. The heart of stone is not exchanged for a heart of flesh. Few are willing to fall upon the Rock and be broken."[3] All, then, must experience repentance, regardless of their disposition or background. "No matter how faultless may have been your lives, as sinners you have steps to take. You are required to repent, believe, and be baptized."[4]

Lukewarm Laodiceans must experience this genuine repentance, this changing and radical redirecting of the mind. This entails a change in habitual, sin-warped mindset; in attitudes, in our perception of life and other people, in our posture toward God and spiritual things. It reaches any inward, secret reserve toward the things of God, any hypocrisy respecting professions of piety, any sense of satisfaction with ourselves, any concealed unwillingness to conform in any way to His standards of righteousness, any rebelliousness lurking on the edges of consciousness.

Isn't Repentance Something We Do?

In categorizing those things that are God's and those things that are ours in the plan of salvation, as we are doing in this book, we might at first decide that repentance is our responsibility. After all, repentance is something that we do, not God.

But Romans 2:4 puts us right: "The goodness of God leads you to repentance."

It is pointed out that "leads" is here used in the sense of conducts. At the right time God, as it were, takes charge and conducts us to repentance, to which we could never arrive did He not do so. Thus, like drawing and convicting, repentance is from God. "Repentance is the gift of God, and whom He pardons He first makes penitent."[5] The natural heart feels no need of repentance; indeed, *cannot* feel a need of repentance. "Repentance is no less the gift of God than are pardon and justification, and it cannot be experienced except as it is given to the soul by Christ."[6]

So God instills in our minds and hearts the disposition to repentance. We must act on that impulse as the disposition is with us. It will not last if we do not do our part.

The effect of repentance is not primarily and most importantly on the feelings, as many seem to think. For repentance to be genuine it must be more deep-rooted and stable than feelings can be by their very nature. So repentance has to involve the faculties of the mind. If it were primarily of the feelings, it would be as changeable as the feelings may be changeable. So our repentance could then be heartfelt and determined one hour, and wavering and doubtful the next, as indeed it appears to be with some people.

For this reason, God wisely has made repentance principally a matter of the mind and heart, for these faculties are so constituted that in the normal individual they are more focused and stable than feelings, and are the repository of reason, judgment, motive and volition, as opposed to mere emotion. They may be compared to an island in the sea as contrasted with the sea itself, now calm, now stormy.

So genuine repentance is not to be a one-time, passing sentiment, but continuing and consistent, a settled decision of mind. It is not dependent on emotions but on convictions based on our knowledge of God's will for us.

"A repentance caused by a spasmodic exercise of the feelings is a repentance that needs to be repented of; for it is delusive. A violent exercise of the feelings, which does not produce in you the peaceable fruits of righteousness, leaves you in a worse state than you were in before."[7] "The life we live is to be one of continual repentance and humility. We need to repent constantly, that we may be constantly victorious."[8]

Repentance is a Change of Mind

Repentance, then, has to do essentially with the mind. It is first and foremost, to note the literal meaning of the Greek word, "a change of mind." This does not mean a mere change of opinion but of intention, of attitude. It is a redirecting of the will.

Repentance is more a matter of sorrow for *sin* than for *sins*.

What do I mean by this?

Have you ever had one of those sudden, perceptive, clear-sighted moments when you suddenly saw yourself as you knew you really were—base, corrupted, vile? Have you ever felt a deep-down, all-pervasive disgust with yourself, and known a judgment of conscience telling you you are utterly iniquitous? Repelled by yourself, have you ever asked, Why am I the way I am? Why do I have these attitudes? Why do I feel this way? Why do I say those kinds of things, do those kinds of things? I'm fed up with myself.

Do you ever feel as Peter felt, "Depart from me, for I am a sinful man, O Lord"? At the time, his reaction was not because he may have committed some particular sin. Peter here illustrates what I mean by repentance being more a sorrow for sin as a principle, as a fundamental condition of the heart, than *sins,* those thoughts, words, acts, that flow from the condition.

In this condition one feels devastated more by what he is than by what he has done. He experiences the need of a radical, bedrock changing of himself. So the repentance God offers brings a longing, not only for forgiveness, but for a purifying of the heart from which those things that need forgiveness, issue, that they may be choked at the source.

When we realize this need, and submit to it, all barriers between us and God come down. There is no more defensiveness, no more self-justification. We are willing to be totally vulnerable before Him. We will hide nothing, defend nothing, keep nothing.

Repentance is Much More Than a Wave of Emotion

It is easy to feel sorry for the wrong one has done; yet this feeling may not carry with it any determination not to repeat the wrong. A wave of emotion may sweep over the soul, and during its passage all love of sin may be buried, and only the most becoming ideas appear on the surface. But they will be but froth and foam melting into nothing, and they will vanish with the retreating wave, leaving the hard rock beneath quite unmoved. There is no real repentance until the will is touched, until the penitent resolves to abandon his sin and to seek a better life. He may well see that he cannot do this himself; his sin is too strong for him, and the better life is above his reach. Repentance is not regeneration, but is a sincere desire for a new life, an honest determination to seek it.[9]

But this imperative is beyond us personally. "The natural heart feels no need of repentance."[10]

In repentance, we cease to war with God and with conscience.

In the October 21, 1884, *Review and Herald,* Ellen White wrote of the Laodicean condition of the people at a particular camp meeting, but then made a broader application:

> As a people we are in imminent danger; for we are becoming superficial, deficient in practical godliness. In our camp meetings we never receive the blessing that it is our privilege to gain; for we cease our efforts too soon. There is some confessing in a general way; but the real evil is untouched. There is no sense of the hatefulness of sin. There is repenting without brokenness of heart; there is professing to leave the world, but the life is still governed by its principles.

Christ's Emphasis: Repentance

We are often inclined to emphasize revival and reformation. But Christ emphasized repentance. Without repentance we can never have a genuine revival and reformation. Revival and reformation will follow repentance. Without repentance the Latter Rain cannot come. "If we would be saved at last we must all learn the lesson of penitence and faith at the foot of the cross."[11]

> We often sorrow because our evil deeds bring unpleasant consequences to ourselves; but this is not repentance. Real sorrow for sin is the result of the working of the Holy Spirit. The Spirit reveals the ingratitude of the heart that has slighted and grieved the Saviour, and brings us in contrition to the foot of the cross. By every sin Jesus is wounded afresh; and as we look upon Him whom we have pierced, we mourn for the sins that have brought anguish upon Him. Such mourning will lead to the renunciation of sin.[12]

Such mourning led to the decision of the prodigal son, "I will arise and go to my Father, and will say to him, 'Father, I have sinned against heaven and before you, and I am no longer worthy to be called your son. Make me like one of your hired servants'" (Luke 15:18, 19). It leads to a similar decision in awakened Laodiceans.

1. Taylor, Richard S., *Exploring Christian Holiness*, (Kansas City, MO: Beacon Hill Press of Kansas City, ©1985), Volume 3, page 173.
2. White, *Our High Calling*, page 82.
3. White, *Testimonies for the Church*, Volume 5, page 218.
4. White, *Testimonies for the Church*, Volume 4, page 40.
5. White, *Selected Messages*, Book 1, page 324.
6. White, Ibid., page 319.
7. White, Ibid., page 108.
8. White, *Seventh-day Adventist Bible Commentary*, Volume 7, page 959.
9. Spence, H. D. M., Excell, Joseph S., editors, *The Pulpit Commentary*, Grand Rapids: William B. Eerdmans Publishing Company, ©1961), Volume 5, page 82.
10. White, *Review and Herald*, December 1, 1904.
11. White, *Lift Him Up*, page 240.
12. White, *The Desire of Ages*, page 300.

Chapter 8
Our Part: Confess

People who receive the latter rain will have responded to God's draw-ing, freely acknowledged their sinfulness and needs and, in repen-tance, will have confessed their sins and their sinfulness. They will have committed everything wholly to God that He might justify and then transform them by the readying early rain.

He who covers his sins will not prosper, but whoever confesses and forsakes them will have mercy (Proverbs 28:13).

God offers us repentance. Accepting that gift wholeheartedly means confession and surrender and a turning away from sin resolutely.

More is embraced in repentance and confession than many of us real-ize. Christ used an illustration that invokes the visual and the sensory. Ellen White also uses this illustration to help us perceive what genuine, full re-pentance and confession mean.

Picture someone standing on a stone ledge on a mountain stumbling and falling one hundred and fifty feet to a large rock below. Visualize him plummeting through the air. Sense him landing, with sickening impact, broken, on the rock.

The image is not a pleasant one. We may even resent a little being asked to fancy it. But it vividly suggests what must happen, spiritually, to you and me if we are to be born again, to be sanctified by the early rain. Then we might receive the latter rain and by it be readied to do the last work the church is called to do. And we will be prepared to stand through the seven last plagues.

Matthew 21:44 records the brief illustration used by Jesus: "Whoever falls on this Stone will be broken; but on whomever It falls, It will grind him to powder." The very fact that Jesus used this illustration of being broken on a rock, tells us that real repentance, confession, and surrender is hard, painful. It involves inward violence, a putting to death of self, a dying to self, and this is hard.

What Dying to Self Means

Dying to self tells us that self, that reservoir of pride, self-esteem, self-righteousness, self-dignity, pretentiousness, must be shattered, broken in pieces, before we can be remade after the image of the Master.

That prideful self which secretly assures us we are superior to another person. That willful independence which may in appearance obey God, perhaps because of expedience, but which inwardly is unsubmissive. That concealed worldliness which permits the ears and eyes and thoughts to lean toward unchristlike things when they come into the perimeter of our attention. That spiritual self-sufficiency which refuses to countenance the suggestion that my "whole head is sick, and the whole heart faints," that "from the sole of the foot even to the head, there is no soundness in it, but wounds and bruises and putrefying sores; [that] they have not been closed or bound up, or soothed with ointment" (Isaiah 1:5, 6). That arrogance which makes ourselves the arbiters of what is right and what is wrong, what is allowable and what is not, rather than bowing to a "thus saith the Lord." That oft-rising peevishness, that over-fondness for money, that vanity which fishes for the admiration of others, that self-interest which is allowed to stifle the Spirit's efforts to make us put the needs of others before our own.

We could go on and on. The list is virtually endless.

We hope that once again the idea has begun to strike home that there is a more serious problem than the confession of individual transgressions. There is a problem with us as human beings. There is a wholesale involvement of our natures in sin. As salt infuses the whole recipe, so sin is infused through our beings. All is affected. Thus a true confession encompasses not just what we have *done* but what we *are*. As we have emphasized previously, we have come to understand that we have not only committed acts of sin, but that we are sinners. In fact, even though we may appear to have lived impeccable lives, as the rich young ruler apparently did, we are still spiritually corrupt in heart. Therefore we need more than forgiveness. We, every one of us if we have not been changed, need to be changed. This is why Jesus insisted to another seemingly exemplary individual, "Most assuredly, I say to you, unless one is born again, he cannot see the kingdom of God" (John 3:3).

On one occasion Martin Luther exclaimed in deep anguish to his superior in the Augustinian order, Dr. Staupitz, "My sin! My sin! My sin!" yet he was unable to name any particular sin. Luther came to realize that "there is . . . something more drastically wrong with man than any particular list of offenses which can be enumerated, confessed, and forgiven. The very nature of man is corrupt. . . . Luther had come to perceive that the entire man is in need of forgiveness."[1]

Believers "are to fall upon the Rock and be broken." Christ Himself is that Rock (Romans 9:33; 1 Peter 2:7, 8; Isaiah 8:14). "Submission to Christ and faith in Him are here represented. To fall upon the Rock and be broken is to give up our self-righteousness and to go to Christ with the humility of a child, repenting of our transgressions, and believing in His forgiving love."[2]

No Excuses, No Self-justification

In confessing we sometimes tend to place an element of blame upon others or upon circumstances, which betrays the fact that we are not really accepting the full responsibility for our sins.

Referring to one person, Ellen White wrote, "To every acknowledgment of his guilt he adds an apology in excuse of his course, declaring that if it had not been for certain circumstances, he would not have done this or that for which he is reproved. But the examples in God's word of genuine repentance and humiliation reveal a spirit of confession in which there is no excuse for sin or attempt at self-justification."[3]

Genuine confession is like saying, as we stand at the bar of conscience and of God, "OK, God. I'm going to come clean. I'm not going to hold back anything. I want you to know everything. Here's the whole sorry story, the whole messy situation. I'm fully to blame. But, God, you know I'm deeply remorseful about the whole thing. Will you forgive me?"

The General Versus the Specific

It is relatively easy to confess in a general way. For instance, I may say to a friend or a family member, "If I have wronged you, will you forgive?" In this confession there may be the implication, I don't really feel I wronged you. Or if I did, it was no big deal. But if you think I did, I would like for you to forgive me.

Or I may imply, Yes, there is a problem, but the fault may have been, or was, as much yours as mine. Or even more yours than mine. Thus I subtly reduce the blame that should have been mine. And doing this enables me to salve my conscience with the idea that I have done my part in confessing, when I have not really done so at all. In fact, I may have made it worse by placing guilt upon you.

It is hard to frankly confess, "I lied to you when I said. . . ." Or "I blamed you for causing me to lose my temper. But, really, it was my fault."

It is hard to confess because pride must be humbled to do so. And pride tends to paralyze the will, thicken the tongue, and inhibit every move towards confession and restitution.

Moreover, confession sometimes makes it necessary to reveal to others ethical and moral flaws we would just as soon they did not know about. It manifests that we have not always been the good, or honest, or virtuous ones we would like others to think we are.

Sometimes we are ashamed to confess. Perhaps we have needed to admit the same offense two or three or more times previously, and are now embarrassed to have to confess to either God or the one we have wronged.

If this is a problem, let us recall, first, that so far as forgiving is concerned, God does not concentrate on numbers.

Remember Jesus' response to Peter when the disciple asked if he should forgive a wrong seven times? Jesus answered, "I do not say to you, up to seven times, but up to seventy times seven" (Matthew 18:22). In this He reflected the attitude of His Father regarding forgiveness.

Secondly, embarrassment cannot be the criterion as to whether we are to confess or not. Heaven will be worth a little embarrassment.

For reasons such as this "There are many professed Christians whose confessions of sin are similar to that of Achan. They will, in a general way, acknowledge their unworthiness, but they refuse to confess the sins whose guilt rests upon their conscience, and which have brought the frown of God upon His people. Thus many conceal sins of selfishness, over-reaching, dishonesty toward God and their neighbor, sins in the family, and many others which it is proper to confess in public."[4]

So confess we must, in true sincerity, and in specifics, if we are to have the forgiveness of God and the blessings of God.

In connection with certain sin offerings in Leviticus 5, we read that "it shall be, when he is guilty in any of these matters, that he shall confess that he has sinned in that thing" (verse 5). Of this the *Seventh-day Adventist Bible Commentary* observes, "A general confession will not suffice. It must be a confession of 'that thing.' Nothing less will do."[5]

"True confession," Ellen White wrote, "is always of a specific character, and acknowledges particular sins. They may be of such a nature as to be brought before God only; they may be wrongs that should be confessed to individuals who have suffered injury through them; or they may be of a public character, and should then be as publicly confessed. But all confession should be definite and to the point, acknowledging the very sins of which you are guilty."[6] Anything less casts doubt on the genuineness of one's repentance.

Most importantly, confession of *all* sin must be made to God. It must be made from "a broken and a contrite heart," which God will not despise (Psalm 51:17).

Genuine confession of sin occasioned by real repentance brings a forsaking of sin and victory over sin. It is possible to confess sins again and again, but not to put them away by sincere repentance.

Restitution

While I was in academy anther student approached me and confessed that a year or two before he had stolen a book from me. I had no problem forgiving him, but he did not return the book, or offer to replace it.

Yet one vital aspect of confession is restitution. This is a biblical requirement.

> Then the LORD spoke to Moses, saying, "Speak to the children of Israel: 'When a man or woman commits any sin that men commit in unfaithfulness against the LORD, and that person is guilty, then he shall confess the sin which he has done. He shall make restitution for his trespass in full value plus one-fifth of it, and give it to the one he has wronged.' " (Numbers 5:5–7).

With sincere confession comes surrender, for the decision to confess to God, to make things right with everyone, bursts the chains that held us, and we are liberated. At that moment we become free from the heavy weight of guilt. The spiritual freedom and buoyancy that comes with surrender is because we no longer are carrying the load ourselves. Jesus has assumed it. "Therefore if the Son makes you free, you shall be free indeed" (John 8:36).

In our confessing, perhaps we need to acknowledge to God that we have not taken seriously the word of the True Witness, who tells us the condition most of us are in (Revelation 3:15–18), but to whom we have paid scant attention.

Confession, it has been pointed out, was a precondition for all sacrifices made in the Levitical system.[7] The sacrifice was not acceptable to God except as confession for known sin was made before the animal was killed. The sacrifice did not take the place of confession. Its purpose was to provide remission for *confessed* sin only. (Unrecognized, and so unconfessed, sins were covered by the morning and evening sacrifices. These burnt sacrifices provided a temporary and provisional atonement until the sinner recognized his sin. So the robe of Christ's righteousness covers unrecognized sins. See Ellen White Comments, *Seventh-day Adventist Bible Commentary*, Volume 1, page 713.)

Antitypically, then, Christ's sacrifice does not substitute for confession, and it cannot be effectual for us until we confess our known sins. Only confessed sins are remitted by His sacrifice. Thus we cannot be justified with known, unconfessed sins in the life. "Christ's righteousness covers no sin unrepented of."[8]

1. Bainton, Roland H., *Here I Stand: A Life of Martin Luther,* (New York: Mentor Books, ©1955), page 41.
2. White, Ellen G., *The Desire of Ages,* page 599.
3. White, *Testimonies for the Church,* Volume 5, page 641.
4. White, *Seventh-day Adventist Bible Commentary,* Volume 2, page 997.
5. Volume 1, page 735.
6. White, *Steps to Christ,* page 38.
7. Wallenkampf, Arnold V., Lesher, W. Richard, editors, *The Sanctuary and the Atonement,* (Washington, DC: Review and Herald Publishing Association, ©1981), page 97.
8. White, *Seventh-day Adventist Bible Commentary,* Volume 7, page 931.

Chapter 9
God's Part:
He Will Forgive

*P*eople who receive the latter rain will be penitent ones whom God will delight to forgive. His forgiveness, a factor preparatory to the former rain, is a first step in clearing the way for the imparting of the latter rain when God shall choose to send it.

God is very eager to forgive us our sins. "For You, Lord, are good, and ready to forgive, and abundant in mercy to all those who call upon You" (Psalm 86:5). "And the Lord passed before Him [Moses] and proclaimed, The Lord, the LORD God, merciful and gracious, . . . forgiving iniquity and transgression and sin" (Exodus 34:6, 7). "If You, LORD, should mark iniquities [and not be a forgiving God], O Lord, who could stand? But there is forgiveness with You" (Psalm 130:3, 4). "To the Lord our God belong mercy and forgiveness, though we have rebelled against Him" (Daniel 9:9).

Forgiveness is God's way of grace by which He removes the impediments between us and Himself.

By now we understand that forgiveness is not a simple matter. God's justice, His character, the destiny of His whole universe, is tied up with how and why He forgives. His justice must be maintained in every respect. Therefore forgiveness is not simply a situation in which we ask, and He generously pardons. It is not like a child doing something wrong and the parent forgiving with no stipulations involved, and all is well.

Forgiveness has cost God more than we can ever conceive—the life of His Son. Because of the Sacrifice, man and God can meet at the "mercy seat," the place of forgiveness; "The meeting place," as William Temple puts it, "of God's holy love and man's sin."[1]

The German writer, Heinrich Heine, made an oft-quoted remark about God's forgiveness. Confined to his bed with an incurable spinal disease, he nevertheless exhibited a casual unconcern about the future and eternity. Asked why he was so confident, he cynically replied, "God will forgive. It is His trade."

But God cannot forgive so easily. For one thing, from the perspective of the one forgiven, an easy forgiveness is demoralizing. This may be illustrated by what is going on in our justice system. Someone commits a crime, but is let off with a light sentence, or none. This gives him, and others, the idea that what he has done is not so serious after all. Thus there is no deterrence to his committing the same crime again, or another crime.

The conditions God places on forgiveness not only lead the sinner to a genuine repentance for his sin, but will make him realize the seriousness of sin, and so he becomes more sensitive to it.

God's way "is broad enough to receive the greatest sinner if he repents, and it is so narrow, so holy, lifted up so high, that sin cannot be admitted there."[2]

"The unconditional pardon of sin never has been, and never will be."[3] Forgiveness, then, is not contingent on simply asking. It is contingent upon, and always associated with, humility, submission, repentance, confession of sins, and forgiveness of others (Matthew 18:35). We can be forgiven only as we meet these conditions. The parable of the Pharisee and the publican demonstrates this (Luke 18:9–14).

So God always looks at the heart. He examines the basis of repentance. Do we seek it because we shrink from the results of sin, or because we have a real sense of how we have wronged God?

God's forgiveness is more than His wiping the slate clean. When I seek forgiveness the goal is not only that God will pardon my transgressions. It is also that the alienation my sins have brought between God and I be eliminated; that there be a restoration of fellowship and communion. And this is only possible as the sinner is changed as well as forgiven. When the sinner is forgiven, he is also changed.

No Cloak for Unrepented Sins

"The righteousness of Christ is not a cloak to cover unconfessed and unforsaken sin; it is a principle of life that transforms the character and controls the conduct."[4] (In this single sentence is a clear, compact definition of righteousness by faith.)

If we *confess* our sins, He is faithful and just to forgive us our
sins and to cleanse us from all unrighteousness" (1 John 1:9).

It is the confession of our known sins that makes us clean in the eyes of
Him who is Holiness Absolute.[5]

To suggest, then, that we may be forgiven without genuine repentance
is to misrepresent the teachings of the Bible and lower the standards of the
church. And, of course, it is a given that if we sincerely repent, we com-
pletely abandon our sins, and by grace live a righteous life.

We need to consider for a moment what is involved in the cleansing
which comes with confession and forgiveness. First, it is *we* who are cleansed.
It is not simply a celestial register that is wiped free of our record of sins. It
is a personal experience. God cleanses *us.*

In the New Testament uncleanness is a moral condition (Matthew 23:25–
27; Mark 7:14–23); cleansing has to do with that moral condition. At cleansing, which means regeneration, the experiencing of the new birth, the heart
is purified and the mental and moral nature renewed in godliness (Acts
15:9; Psalm 51:10). This assurance of cleansing by the Spirit gives us bold-
ness through Christ to "draw near with a true heart" to the throne of God
(Hebrews 10:19–22).

With Repentance We Are Justified

The title of our chapter has to do with forgiveness. But forgiveness and
justification are actually the same thing. So when we experience this repentance we have been talking about, God forgives, cleanses, regenerates. And
with that act we receive what is theologically termed justification.

What is justification? Expressed simply, it is all the perfection of Jesus
Christ superseding our imperfections when we repent of our sinfulness
and sins and surrender to Christ. Ellen White says in *Steps to Christ,*

> If you give yourself to Him, and accept Him as your Saviour,
> then, sinful as your life may have been, for His sake you are
> accounted righteous. Christ's character stands in place of your
> character, and you are accepted before God just as if you had
> not sinned.[6]

This is justification. But is this all there is to justification?

There has been much debate in the religious world as to whether justification is only judicial; or whether it is also personal, in the sense that there
is something that is done to the individual on the inside.

For a long time it was taught in Protestantism that justification is only judicial. In other words, upon accepting Christ, the penitent is recorded in the books of heaven as being faultless, but that justification has no subjective effect on the individual himself. However, in recent years there has been a swing away from this view on the part of some theologians because they have come to realize that it is *both* judicial and personal. For example, the respected scholar, writer, and evangelist, John R. W. Stott, avers that the biblical teaching that we are justified *in* Christ "makes it impossible for us to think of justification as a purely external transaction; it cannot be isolated from our union with Christ and all the benefits this brings."[7]

Justification: Forgiveness for Sin, Reclaiming from Sin

Ellen White gives the words quoted above from *Steps to Christ* as a definition of justification, but she is clear that this is not all that is involved. "God's forgiveness [forgiveness and justification are 'one and the same thing,'[8]] is not merely a judicial act by which He sets us free from condemnation. It is not only forgiveness *for* sin, but reclaiming *from* sin. It is the outflow of redeeming love that transforms the heart."[9]

We read in the paragraph immediately following the quotation from *Steps to Christ* noted above: "More than this, Christ changes the heart," thus adding the subjective effects of justification.

In his letter to Titus, Paul tells us justification follows regeneration, the new birth, which is "renewal in the Holy Spirit," and which signifies a great change in the sinner.

Our God, Paul writes, "saved us, not because of deeds done by us in righteousness, but in virtue of His own mercy, by the washing of regeneration and renewal in the Holy Spirit, which He poured out upon us richly through Jesus Christ our Savior, *so that we might be justified* by His grace and become heirs in hope of eternal life" (Titus 3:5–7, RSV). [Italics supplied.]

Justification and the New Man

"Justification," the *Seventh-day Adventist Bible Commentary* tells us, is "the cleansing and putting on of the new man 'created in ... holiness' (Ephesians 4:24)."[10] So we must understand that the experience of justification does not leave us the same people we were before, merely credited with being clean while we are actually unchanged. Justification is two-pronged.

At the same time that we are regarded by God as having never sinned, because Jesus' sinless life is now counted as ours; justification effects a renewal of the heart so that we are different people than we were before.

Last, but certainly not least, justification means freedom. In sin the heart, the mind, the will, the body, are bound (Romans 6:18, 20, 22; 8:2; Galatians 5:1). In forgiveness, the bonds are severed.

John Stott mentions four things we are free from in Christ:[11]

1. *The tyranny of the law.* The conscientious person who, like Paul (Romans 7:7–11, 24), glimpses something of the depth and extent of obedience the law demands, and then sets about to meet those demands in his own sinful condition, finds that while the demands of the law are obligatory they are also impossible to fulfill. He can never satisfy them. The law becomes a despot to him, as it did to Paul and to Martin Luther.

In Christ's forgiveness, or justification, there is release from legalism. Legalism is trying to obey God's law without understanding that the power to obey the law comes only from God. In legalism there is no experiencing of that power.

With the forgiveness that comes with repentance and surrender, there comes also empowering for obedience, as well as harmony with the law. Then, "I delight to do Your will, O my God, and Your law is within my heart" (Psalm 40:8). The law then is no longer a tyrant, but a friendly guide which keeps me on the path to heaven.

2. *The tyranny of the flesh.* This may perhaps be best understood when considered in the way Paul frequently uses the term *flesh*. In his terminology it may be seen as sin-impaired human nature operating through a physical body and body faculties whose appetites and passions, impulses and sensibilities are gone awry, weakened and perverted as a result of sin. These faculties consequently afford sin a base from which it can work to misuse and manipulate man. These weakened, perverted faculties make sinful demands, are used by Satan to prompt and entice to sin, and, in spite of ourselves, without Christ to subdue them, they almost always get their way. Thus the flesh tyrannizes over us. (See Romans 6:8–14).

3. *The tyranny of the world.* We may define the term *world* as human society alienated from God and organized under the powers of evil. We are surrounded by the influence of this organization, which is quietly in Satan's hands. That influence, either explicitly or implicitly, tends to make us conform to its thinking which is opposed to Christian thinking. It is that powerful, yet subtle, influence around us against which we are warned in the

oft-quoted Phillips' rendering of Romans 12:2: "Don't let the world around you squeeze you into its own mould."

4. *The tyranny of death*. Death is a foe feared by many. A journalist listed as one of his rules for life, never to think of death. Dr. Samuel Johnson observed that the fear of death is so naturally ingrained into humanity that life is one long effort to keep it at bay. But in triumphant words that through the centuries have echoed hope and confidence, Paul spoke for all Christians, "Death is swallowed up in victory. O death, where is thy sting? O grave, where is thy victory?" (1 Corinthians 15:54, 55, KJV).

1. *Christian Faith and Life*, (London: SCM Press, ©1963), page 84.
2. White, Ellen G., *Selected Messages*, Book 1, page 184.
3. White, *God's Amazing Grace*, page 73.
4. White, *The Desire of Ages*, page 555, 556.
5. White, *Testimonies for the Church*, Volume 1, page 156.
6. Page 62.
7. *The Cross of Christ*, (Downers Grove, IL: Intervarsity Press, ©1986), page 191.
8. White, *Seventh-day Adventist Bible Commentary*, Volume 6, page 1070.
9. White, *Thoughts from the Mount of Blessing*, page 114.
10. Volume 6, page 880.
11. Stott, Op. Cit., page 241f.

Chapter 10
Our Part:
Take God at His Word

People who receive the latter rain will have known the forgiveness, cleansing, justification, and empowering of God for victory through the early rain. They will have learned confidence in His here-and-now ability to give them mastery over self and sin. Without that belief and experience it is impossible for God to open the channel to pour His latter-rain power upon us.

Our faith, our belief, is the foundation on which God perfects His transforming work in our hearts, yet faith is perhaps the hardest trait for human beings to cultivate and practice.

As sinners we must believe that upon our submission to Him, God forgives, accepts, cleanses, and transforms us; and we must act upon that belief. But "here is where thousands fail," Ellen White wrote in connection with our accepting that forgiveness, and living victoriously by faith in God's grace. "They do not believe that Jesus pardons them personally, individually. They do not take God at His word."[1]

Our greatest sin is unbelief in God.[2]

The greatest sin we can cherish is the sin of unbelief.[3]

Every failure on the part of the children of God is due to their lack of faith.[4] [Italics supplied.]

Without faith [belief] it is impossible to please Him (Hebrews 11:6).

Whatever is not from faith [belief] is sin (Romans 14:23).

But before we get into a discussion of the "bad news"—unbelief—let us think about the "good news"—belief.

Belief, Simple and Powerful

Understanding belief in the Christian context, in which it is another term for faith, requires no profound theological definition. Multiplying words to try to help us understand may not really be very helpful. Usually, it is not definitions we need so much as to act on what we already understand.

Belief, or faith, is simply taking God at His word, and proceeding to follow up on it. This is the pith and sum and substance of it all.

This is why, in writing of the forgiving and cleansing of sin, Ellen White penned,

> Faith is simple in its operation and powerful in its results. Many professed Christians, who have a knowledge of the sacred Word, and believe its truth, fail in the childlike trust that is essential to the religion of Jesus. They do not reach out with that peculiar touch that brings the virtue of healing to the soul.[5]

After a moment of reflection on this statement, it becomes apparent that Bible belief cannot be separated from decision and action. As the *Seventh-day Adventist Bible Commentary* observes, "To believe on the name of Jesus is to appropriate the provisions of salvation in Christ Jesus."[6]

The provisions of salvation are not merely legal but living, vital. There is transformation as well as forgiveness. God cleanses, or purifies, as well as pardons (1 John 1:9).

The "peculiar touch" Ellen White writes about has to do with the fact that ultimately belief, or faith, is not dependent on objective evidence which the hard, empirical, modern mind demands. That evidence is available and to a degree is important. But faith takes over where knowledge and proofs come to their limits. More telling than these is the persuasion of the Holy Spirit. His persuasion does not rely on intellectual facts to convince, but upon a conviction that is more comprehensive and compelling, and that goes deeper than the intellect. The Spirit speaks not with words but with "sighs too deep for words" (Romans 8:26, RSV), that are far more persuasive than human language.

The Knowledge of the Soul

The speaking of the Spirit is to the "heart," which includes the whole subjective inner life, the moral center of the personality, the entire disposition, the inner man. Mildred Wynkoop points out that "Jesus said it was out of the *heart* that evil proceeded and it was the *heart* which was to love God wholly. Paul speaks of the *heart* as being darkened and foolish and lustful and hard and impenitent (Romans 1, 2), and the *heart* into which the Holy Spirit sheds love (Romans 5). To him it is the *heart* that obeys (Romans 6:17) and the *heart* that believes (Romans 10:9) unto righteousness."[7] [Italics in original.]

The Spirit does not override reason and facts, or overpower the human will. It superimposes upon them something that is superior to human reason and offers to the will alluring inducements to submit the soul to its Savior.

For the Christian the evidence is and must be more of the heart than of the mind.

> Faith results in spiritual knowledge. By faith we are encouraged to grasp still more; for we behold God in the promise, and are armed with stability. The true Christian knows in whom he believes. He has the evidence of things unseen; and a knowledge that is regenerating, overpowering, follows this. This may not be believed by skeptics, but it is to the receiver no speculation, no mere theory. The Gospel offers to him a remedy for the moral disorders which sin has caused. He does not merely read the Bible, but experiences the Bible. He has not merely heard of the righteousness of Christ; by faith he has opened the windows of his soul to the Sun of Righteousness. Skeptics may stand back and argue the impossibility of the remedy he has taken, but their words are nothing to him against experience. It is a matter of knowledge with him.[8]

The Anatomy of Unbelief

We have defined belief as taking God at His word and acting upon it. The flip side is that unbelief is *not* taking God at His word.

Unbelief is not and cannot be linked with ignorance. It is nonsensical to say, "I don't know anything about the matter; therefore I don't believe it." Unbelief is a rejection of some aspect of knowledge.

Unbelief is not the same as doubt. Strictly speaking, there are two categories of doubt. There is the honest intellectual sort leading to a suspension of opinion because of a lack of knowledge. This doubt may start one on a search for truth.

Then there is the more common kind which is skepticism that seems to be less of the mind than of the heart. Its source is the same as that of unbelief. It springs from pride or cynicism, a bias of interest, or an attachment to opinions or practices that seem too attractive, or too adhesive, to be escaped.

This doubt is not outright unbelief. It is a deep shadow falling across faith. It is a condition in which one teeters between belief and unbelief, while leaning toward unbelief.

Unbelief, on the other hand, is doubt that has crossed the line. It no longer teeters. It has essentially dismissed belief and is converted to skepticism. It is disbelief, a refusal to believe. It is a condition of the heart (Hebrews 3:12), a moral state.

Biblically, unbelief is a refusal to go by the evidence, commands, or promises God presents. So it looks for arguments, not to refute its skepticism, but to make it more plausible. It is choosing to follow one's own judgment, often because it is more pleasing to the ego. It is choosing one's own position, perhaps because it is more agreeable to the lifestyle one chooses to follow.

Unbelief in God is a moral issue. By moral we mean, simplistically, that it has to do with truth and error, right and wrong, good and bad, fairness and unfairness. We may illustrate as follows: Suppose that your spouse, or your best friend, has proved time and time again, "through thick and thin," over thirty years, that they are dependable, and will not let you down. Yet suppose you still did not believe they were trustworthy, and you acted out that unbelief. Wouldn't this mistrust demonstrate a serious moral flaw in you, rather than a fault in them? Would you be fair to them? Would you be doing right by them?

> Know that the LORD your God, He is God, the faithful God, who keeps covenant (Deuteronomy 7:9).
>
> Great is Thy faithfulness (Lamentations 3:23, KJV).
>
> He who promised is faithful (Hebrews 10:23).

If we believe not, yet He abideth faithful: He cannot deny Himself (2 Timothy 2:13, KJV).

So when we demonstrate a lack of faith in God, of whom there is none more trustworthy, nor can there be, we are manifesting the most serious moral outrage.

Our distrust [of God] is an insult to the One who has done so much for us.[9]

Fundamentally, then, in religion, unbelief is not believing in God, a Person, the infinitely trustworthy One. It is more serious to disbelieve in a person than in an idea. It is infinitely more serious to disbelieve in God rather than in our own dark unbelief.

The two common Greek words in the New Testament translated *unbelief,* and various terms suggesting the idea, signify disobedience; or a refusal to be persuaded; or distrust. It is an absence of faith. It is the heart's refusal to place confidence in God. It is the will's rejection of the evidence He presents.

In the words of the *Beacon Dictionary of Theology,* unbelief "is the moral resistance to, and lack of confidence in, the commands and promises of God, which arise from an evil heart (Hebrews 3:12)."[10]

A False Sanctification

There was a day when Adventists were strong on performance (which was called sanctification) and weak on justification. We have made a wide swing in the last few decades so that now we are strong on what is termed justification, at the expense of sanctification.

But what was thought to be sanctification by many was a false sanctification that deceived them as surely as the Jews Paul wrote of in Romans 10. They had a "zeal for God, but not according to knowledge. For they being ignorant of God's righteousness, and seeking to establish their own righteousness, have not submitted to the righteousness of God" (verses 2, 3).

The sad fact is that some of us have been more deceived than the Jews because the Jews believed they could be made righteous by keeping the law. We have in theory maintained we are not so saved, but in practice have followed the same path they have.

This fact is vividly brought home to me as I think of a young married couple I was acquainted with in my academy days. They were leaders in church activities, and were regarded as the ideal Christian couple, a model for other young people.

Then, abruptly, they announced they were throwing everything overboard and leaving the church. They dumped all Adventist lifestyle scruples and plunged into the social life of the world.

It was reported that after they took that step the woman said, "I have never been so free in all my life."

That statement tells it all. It is crystal clear that for whatever reason—lack of understanding, an unwillingness to make a thorough commitment—they had not reached out "with that peculiar touch that brings the virtue of healing to the soul."[11] Instead, "While they think they are committing themselves to God, there is a great deal of self-dependence. There are conscientious souls that trust partly to God, and partly to themselves. They do not look to God, to be kept by His power, but depend upon watchfulness against temptation, and the performance of certain duties for acceptance with Him. There are no victories in this kind of faith."[12]

Accepting Assurance Without Victory

So, many of us settle for another solution—assurance without the kind of victory pledged in our Bibles and in the Spirit of Prophecy writings. We do not by faith take hold of the dimension of victory promised. Many do not believe God's grace may make them victors over all their sins; they see the only solution to their sin problem as being justification without victory. They do not see the possibility, or perhaps even the importance, of the transformed life. They find assurance in imputed righteousness as they understand it. Thus we find many church members whose lifestyles are not significantly different from many who live "in the world," as we say.

Religious belief is largely a matter of the will, of choice. In chapter six we related the story of the atheist who, in spite of all evidence for the resurrection of Christ, insisted that he would not believe. Clearly, he chose to not believe despite the evidence weighed heavily on the side of belief.

There is another area of unbelief that is more serious than this for it casts reflection on the saving ability of the Savior. For even when He is preached and believed on as a pardoning Savior, He is ofttimes presented as an objective Redeemer, not as one who dwells within and actually cleanses the heart of all unrighteousness.

Faith that takes hold only of forgiveness but cannot encompass cleansing, power and victory, is an inadequate faith. It is possible to accept forgiveness intellectually and extrapolate this mental concept as an act of faith, when it may be nothing more than, and limited to, the intellectual. If we do not have that "peculiar touch," we find techniques by which we are able to persuade ourselves that all is well, and to rationalize the evidence of the failures which could have been victories, had we taken hold in full faith.

It is easy, superficially, to say we believe that God objectively forgives us of our sins. Multitudes make the profession, in whom there is little subsequent sign that they are any different than before they made it. In fact, most of what is today termed Christianity does not really expect much difference when one supposedly becomes a Christian. We are not changed much by so becoming, is the belief. (I read somewhere of an Adventist college student who remarked, "We must choose to sin—it is our nature. . . . Our freedom to choose not to sin is regained at the Second Coming.") There is no deep personal commitment, only a nominal subscription to an intellectual creed. So in what way are they distinct from the average person? The only real difference is that now they "believe." But true Christians are "different" in a very real sense, as we have seen.

Because many have not learned the science of experiencing the full and continuing victory over temptation and sin which Christianity can give them (here is the "science of salvation,"[13]) they do not believe it is possible, and it becomes impossible because they do not believe. Thus, as a result of not having the faith to take God at His word, they have trapped themselves in a circular prison—in an attitude which can do nothing but confirm for them the impossibility of overcoming.

---

[1] White, Ellen G., *Steps to Christ,* page 52.
[2] White, *Manuscript Releases,* Volume 4, page 395.
[3] White, *Signs of the Times,* October 4, 1899.
[4] White, *Patriarchs and Prophets,* page 657.
[5] White, *Seventh-day Adventist Bible Commentary,* Volume 6, page 1074.
[6] Volume 5, pages 900, 901.
[7] *A Theology of Love,* (Kansas City, MO: Beacon Hill Press of Kansas City, 1972), page 243.
[8] White, *Signs of the Times,* October 4, 1899.
[9] White, *Review and Herald,* November 19, 1901.
[10] Page 534.
[11] White, *Seventh-day Adventist Bible Commentary,* Volume 6, page 1074.
[12] White, *Selected Messages,* Book 1, page 353.
[13] White, *Fundamentals of Christian Education,* page 187.

Chapter 11
God's Part:
He Will Live In You

The people who receive the latter rain will be experiencing the vital spiritual union with Christ so vividly described in the parable of the vine and the branches.

God's plan is to make known His secret to His people, this rich and glorious secret which He has for all peoples. And the secret is that *Christ is in you* . . . (Colossians 1:27, TEV).

> I bow my knees to the Father of our Lord Jesus Christ, . . . that He would grant you, according to the riches of His glory, to be strengthened with might through His Spirit in the inner man, that Christ may dwell in your hearts through faith (Ephesians 3:14, 16, 17).

> But you are not in the flesh but in the Spirit, if indeed the Spirit of God *dwells in you* (Romans 8:9).

> Examine yourselves as to whether you are in the faith. Prove yourselves. Do you not know yourselves, *that Jesus Christ is in you?*—unless indeed you are disqualified" (2 Corinthians 13:5). [Italics supplied in each quote above.]

"We are slow to believe . . . [that] the likeness of Christ [may] be exhibited in those who are God's sons through Jesus," wrote J. B. Phillips.[1] In fact, in some quarters there is strong opposition to the concept.

Yet, time after time in Ephesians, Paul explicitly or implicitly uses the figure of Christ dwelling in the Christian. We quoted above a few statements from him. (See also Ephesians 3:17, 19; 4:6.)

The fact of the spiritual, mysterious, but nevertheless literal, living relationship between Jesus and the regenerated person is graphically portrayed in John 15. "Christ's connection with His believing people is illustrated by this parable as by no other," writes Ellen White. "By the parable of the true vine, Christ explained to his followers the relation that must exist between him and his people."[2]

Unless there is a genuine, literal, spiritual connection between Christ and His people, the illustration of John 15:1–8 is virtually meaningless. (And this experience is not only for the 144,000. As the above texts demonstrate, it was God's will for His people in Paul's day. It has been His will for His people of all time. Kenneth Strand is probably right in suggesting that the experience of the 144,000 will not be "unique in kind but in intensity."[3])

A Subjective Reality

The portrayal of living, organic bonding of the branches with the vine, the flowing sap and interconnected fibers, and the fruit that comes because the branches are joined to the vine, can only epitomize the subjective reality, and not merely a figurative relationship, that exists between Jesus and His people.

Examine the figure literally for a moment. Here is a grapevine with its many branches absolutely dependent on the vine for life and fruit. That life comes by way of the sap, and only by way of the sap that flows from the vine into the branches. All growth—every bud that bursts, every leaf that greens, every grape that swells, does so because life flows to it by virtue of its constant and living connection with the vine. Once again I emphasize, *the branches' dependence on the vine is real and absolute.*

This, said Jesus to His disciples, is a figure of the relationship between you and Me if you are truly Mine. It is far more than an association of close friends, or of Master and disciple, Teacher and student, even though it is all those things. There is a relationship between us that is absolutely unique, that can be experienced by none who do not consummate that relationship with Me. By My Spirit, Jesus is saying, I will actually make My abode in your hearts. You cannot understand this, only experience it. But it is a reality as surely as this vine and its branches are real.

And because I will dwell in your hearts when you believe I will and when you submit to My loving discipline, then you will show in your lives and characters the same qualities that are seen in Me.

The connection of the branch with the vine, He [Jesus] said, represents the relation you are to sustain to Me. The scion is engrafted into the living vine, and fiber by fiber, vein by vein, it grows into the vine stock. The life of the vine becomes the life of the branch. So the soul dead in trespasses and sins receives life through connection with Christ. By faith in Him as a personal Saviour the union is formed. The sinner unites his weakness to Christ's strength, his emptiness to Christ's fullness, his frailty to Christ's enduring might. Then he has the mind of Christ. The humanity of Christ has touched our humanity, and our humanity has touched divinity. Thus through the agency of the Holy Spirit man becomes a partaker of the divine nature. He is accepted in the Beloved.[4]

Let's look again at the implications of our figure to fix the idea in our minds. The same sap that flows in the vine flows through the branch. Thus the same qualities found in the vine are also in the branch. Any life that shows in the branch is by virtue of the vine. The growth of the branch, its leaves, and the fruit upon it, are there because of the inner life from the vine which flows to it.

Clear Spiritual Implications

Are not the spiritual implications of this illustration clear and unmistakable? For the genuine Christian "it is no longer I who live, but Christ lives in me; and the life which I now live in the flesh I live by faith in the Son of God, who loved me and gave Himself for me" (Galatians 2:20). Thus, if Christ is living in us, *the same kind of life He lived on earth He will now live in us.*

Christianity is lived on the inside. Whatever is seen on the outside is merely a radiation.

The life of Christ in you produces the same fruits as in Him. Living in Christ, adhering to Christ, supported by Christ, drawing nourishment from Christ, you bear fruit after the similitude of Christ.[5]

A. W. Tozer makes a daring comment on this concept:

Just as in eternity God acted like Himself and when incarnated in human flesh still continued in all His conduct to be true to

His holiness, so does He when He enters the nature of a believing man. This is the method by which He makes the redeemed man holy. He enters a human nature at regeneration as He once entered human nature at the incarnation and acts as becomes God, using that nature as a medium of expression for His moral perfection.[6]

Think now about a statement in *Steps to Christ,* page 69, referred to in another chapter: "Many have an idea that they must do some part of the work *alone.* They have trusted in Christ for the forgiveness of sin, but now they seek by their own efforts to live aright. But every such effort must fail. Jesus says, '*Without Me* ye can do nothing.' Our growth in grace, our joy, our usefulness,—all depend upon our union with Christ." [Italics supplied.] The figure of the vine and the branches illustrates how impossible a bisected relationship would be for the Christian. The branches *cannot* of themselves produce fruit. It is impossible. Spiritual fruit is the product of the Spirit (Galatians 5:22, 23), never of ourselves, or even partly of ourselves. That part which we may try to do *on our own* is totally unacceptable to God. And because we thus bring a mixed offering, none is acceptable.

The metaphor of the vine and the branches has been compared with another metaphor: We cannot live unless we are in an environment of air, and the air is in us. So with Christ. Unless we are in Him, and likewise He in us, we cannot live His life—the spiritual life.

> "As many as received Him, to them gave He power to become the sons of God, even to them that believe on His name." John 1:12. This power is not in the human agent. It is the power of God. *When a soul receives Christ, he receives power to live the life of Christ.*[7] [Italics supplied.]

What Does "In Christ" Mean?

As an illustration of the Christian's intimacy, his oneness, with Christ, Paul, in writing to the Corinthians, refers to the sexual relationship between a man and a woman. "Do you not know that your bodies are members of Christ? . . . Do you not know that he who is joined to a harlot is one body with her? For 'The two,' He [God] says, 'shall become one flesh.' But he who is joined to the Lord *is one spirit with Him.*" (1 Corinthians 6:15–17).

In commenting on the words "To the saints ... faithful in Christ" (Ephesians 1:1), the *Tyndale New Testament Commentaries* remark, "As the root is in the soil, the branch in the vine (cf. John 15:1ff), the fish in the sea, the bird in the air, so the place of the Christian's life is in Christ. Physically his life is in the world; spiritually it is lifted above the world to be in Christ."[8]

1. Phillips, J. B., *Making Men Whole,* (London: Fontana Books, ©1959), page 93.
2. *Review and Herald,* September 18, 1900.
3. Noted by George R. Knight, *The Pharisees Guide to Perfect Holiness,* (Boise, ID: Pacific Press Publishing Association, ©1992), page 187.
4. White, *The Desire of Ages,* page 675.
5. White, Ibid., page 677.
6. Tozer, A. W., *A Treasury of A. W. Tozer,* (Grand Rapids, MI: Baker Book House, ©1980), pages 155, 156.
7. White, *Christ's Object Lessons,* page 314.
8. R. V. G. Tasker, Editor, *The Tyndale New Testament Commentaries,* "The Epistle of Paul to the Ephesians" (Grand Rapids: Wm. B. Eerdmans Pub. Co., 1981), page 43.

Chapter 12
Our Part:
Living by Faith

*P*eople who receive the latter rain will have come into union with Christ and will, in His strength and by His grace, be exemplifying Him.

In chapter ten we dealt with *saving* faith as a requisite for the Christian. In this chapter we get into the matter of *living* by that faith a life that is possible as Christ dwells within. With a bit of a shift from James' perspective, we are dealing with his challenge, Show me your faith by your works. James was talking more particularly in an objective sense, about such things as helping orphans and widows, while we are thinking somewhat more subjectively, about having the fruit of the Spirit in the life, "love, joy, peace, longsuffering, kindness, goodness, faithfulness, gentleness, self-control" (Galatians 5:22, 23). Of course, from that subjective experience will spring objective "works." Of this, referring back for the moment to the previous chapter, we read in *The Desire of Ages,* "The life of the vine will be manifest in fragrant fruit on the branches. 'He that abideth in Me,' said Jesus, 'and I in him, the same bringeth forth much fruit: for without Me ye can do nothing.' When we live by faith on the Son of God, the fruits of the Spirit will be seen in our life; not one will be missing."[1]

In the title of this chapter, both the words "living" and "faith" should be given star billing. There is a tendency in some quarters to place almost all the emphasis on "faith," giving "living" only a relatively perfunctory notice. Or, to use terms that are much bandied about these days, some will place the emphasis on justification (by faith) and will depreciate sanctification (which also comes by faith). Actually, as we saw in chapter nine, the sharp division often made between the two is not a biblical one. As the *Seventh-*

day Adventist Bible Commentary points out, "the cleansing and putting on of the new man"[2] comes with justification.

I have just stated that both *living* and *faith* should have star billing. I certainly did not mean that *living*, which in some respects might be equated with James' *works*, could be substituted for, or in the smallest way equal or supplant, *faith*.

It may be taken as a given that I subscribe to the supremacy of faith. There is no substitute for faith. Nothing can displace it. Christianity is meaningless if it is lacking. The future is a dreadful darkness without it. Salvation is a deceptive dream if faith is absent. Profession is a hollow shell if it is wanting. And Christian living is impossible if it is not possessed. Which takes us back to our title, "*Living* by *Faith*."

"The Just Shall Live By Faith"

The great, definitive statement of the Reformation of the sixteenth century was the words of Romans 1:17: "The just shall live by faith." When the significance of these words sank home for Martin Luther, he was as a man suddenly released from intolerable chains. "I felt myself to be reborn and to have gone through open doors into paradise," he wrote.

God gave Luther a glimpse of what he and the world needed at the time, which was to see the beauty and significance of justification. The Christian world was groaning under what was for many the unendurable burden of a system in which one could expect to be right with God only after a long process of meritorious works done through "sacramental" grace. And there could be no real assurance as to when, or if, such works were acceptable to God. Luther had been a slave of such works. He had had a prodigious sense of his sinfulness, and an incessant guilt. And he had pictured God as an unrelenting tyrant, ever watchful to catch him up in a fault, One whom he must appease by penances, vigils, indulgences, fastings, scourgings, and the like. But in these he found no relief.

In that situation Luther needed to see not the requirements of the law, proper though they be, but the grace and love and forgiveness of God. He needed to understand that salvation is not by works of man but by the grace of God; that with respect to justification, we are "justified freely by His grace" (Romans 3:24); that it is "by grace you have been saved through faith, and that not of yourselves; it is the gift of God" (Ephesians 2:8). (Grace may be defined as the divine response to man's inability to do anything about sin and his own fallen nature, in which response is provided for man all that he needs for his forgiveness and salvation but does not deserve. That grace involves not merely justification but also sanctification.)

But so dominant did the judicial aspects of justification become to Luther's followers that they almost entirely lost sight of sanctification. And many Protestants have not, to this day, been able to get the two into proper perspective.

"Luther's doctrine of justification alone (a doctrine heartily endorsed by Calvin) and Calvin's own doctrine of election so emphasized the forensic aspects of salvation as almost to exclude any actual sanctification of the believer."[3]

Because of the need to offset the great emphasis laid upon meritorious works by the church of his day, it is not at all surprising that Luther perceived justification the way he did, seeing only part of the significance of Romans 1:17. He did see what needed stressing at a particular moment. (We may note that Paul in some places also deals with justification in a somewhat similar situation because of a controversy over the function of the law in salvation, hence his particular emphasis.) And since Luther's day many others, following his and other theologians' lead, have missed an important part of that text also.

As I paused a page or two back to underline my conviction in the supremacy of faith, I now accentuate my categorical belief and acceptance of the biblical teaching of *justification* by faith. I wholeheartedly subscribe to the words of Ellen White that "the sweetest melodies that come from God through human lips [are] justification by faith, and the righteousness of Christ."[4] As I ponder the implications of that great kindness for me—a fallen, sinful, naturally rebellious individual, with all my flaws, weaknesses, foibles and failings—I can only feel inadequate gratitude for the gracious favor.

It is noteworthy and significant that the above quotation makes some distinction between "justification by faith" and "the righteousness of Christ."

Sanctification, the Goal of the Gospel

We need to be reminded that experientially the goal, the consummation, of the Gospel is sanctification. "For this is the will of God, your sanctification" (1 Thessalonians 4:3, RSV). And Paul also wrote, "God from the beginning chose you for *salvation through sanctification by the Spirit* and belief in the truth" (2 Thessalonians 2:13). [Italics supplied.]

Hebrews 12:14 makes the indispensable nature of sanctification very definite: "Pursue . . . holiness, *without which no man will see the Lord.*" [Italics supplied.]

The connection of this text with the above may not be apparent to the English reader, but in the Greek the words rendered *sanctification* and *holiness* are identical; thus sanctification and holiness are synonymous. In fact, the *RSV Interlinear Greek-English New Testament* translates Hebrews 12:14, "follow *sanctification*, without which no one will see the Lord."

These texts, emphasizing the place of sanctification, serve in no respect to weaken or displace justification. In its function justification, like faith, stands alone. Nothing can add to it; nothing can take its place. But it is not a passive quality, like some inert gas that creates no change or interaction in that which it contacts.

The scientist uses a particular medium, some nutritive substance, in his laboratory with the aim of growing a desired culture. This substance is absolutely essential to developing that culture. So justification, which is always preceded by regeneration (Titus 3:5–7, RSV), is the essential "medium" in which sanctification grows. It provides the ever-present, indispensable atmosphere, the medium, in which sanctification flowers and flourishes. This is a reason why justification is one of the sweetest melodies flowing from human lips. Sanctification, then, is possible only after one has been justified. It continues always under the power canopy of justification, and it is a result of justification. But also our continuing justification depends, to no small degree, on whether we continue on the path of sanctification. The two work in tandem.

Sanctification without justification, then, and justification without sanctification, are contrary to the Scripture. (We might also observe that sanctification without *faith* is impossible; and faith without *sanctification* is dead.) However, the fact that, as the above texts imply, justification is the medium in which sanctification develops, indicates that the end purpose is indeed sanctification. In the scientist's laboratory the medium is always for the benefit of the culture, not the reverse. Someone has perceptively said that sanctification is "the growing edge" of justification.

Sanctification, a Work of Man or of God?

Perhaps the major reason for the frequent emphasis on justification, making it in some quarters the be-all and end-all of salvation, and the resultant diminution of sanctification, is that justification is seen as an act of God while sanctification is perceived as a work of man, and therefore without particular worth or acceptance with God. This is incorrect. As we observed above, as justification is by faith, so is sanctification.

Before we proceed, we should take a moment to define sanctification. There are two facets to sanctification. One is described by the well-known statement that "sanctification is separation for a holy use." This sanctification, separation, or setting apart, which is done by God, takes place the moment an individual commits himself or herself to God. At that time the individual is justified and cleansed. All things become new (2 Corinthians 5:17). The Greek of texts such as 1 Corinthians 6:11, Ephesians 5:26, and 1 Thessalonians 5:23, describe this "setting apart" aspect.

With that experience there begins in the life the second aspect, a process of spiritual growth. This process is also called sanctification, and is what we are generally referring to when we use the term. This growth—the branch growing and producing leaves and fruit because it partakes of the sap of the vine—is one in which the Christian, working with God, more and more reflects in his life the perfections of Jesus Christ. Texts such as 1 Thessalonians 4:3, Hebrews 2:11 and 1 Peter 1:2, describe this process. Believers are called God's building, which implies an ongoing work—sanctification (Ephesians 2:20; 1 Corinthians 3:9; Colossians 2:7).

So, as by faith we grasp God's promises, He writes His laws in our hearts and makes it possible for us to obey them (Ezekiel 11:19, 20). The Christian way is to walk (live day by day) "according to the Spirit." In this way "the righteous requirement of the law might be fulfilled in us" (Romans 8:4). This is sanctification by faith.

Scripture is replete with texts after this order by which we may illustrate that sanctification is by faith. Sanctification, then, is not a work that man does by himself. It is not man's imperfect work for God, but God's perfecting work in man. As concluded in the previous chapter, it is a result of Christ, received in the life, living His life in us. So man is indeed involved in sanctification, but God much more.

A thoughtful reading of Philippians 2:12, 13 shows on which side the weight of emphasis is in sanctification: "work out your own salvation with fear and trembling; for it is God who works in you both to will and to do for His good pleasure."

J. B. Phillips rendering of verse 13 brings out the primacy of God's part: "For it is God who is at work within you, *giving you the will and the power to achieve His purpose.*" This concept is illuminated by two Spirit of Prophecy quotations, used previously in the Introduction, that contrast our part and

God's part: "The work of the Holy Spirit is immeasurably great."[5] "The part man is required to sustain is immeasurably small, yet in the plan of God it is just that part that is needed to make the work a success. We are laborers together with God. This is the Lord's own wise arrangement. The cooperation of the human will and endeavor with divine energy is the link that binds men up with one another and with God."[6]

In living by faith, then, you and I have a part to play, an absolutely indispensible and active part. We are required to put heart and soul and mind into working out our own salvation. But our all is still negligible when contrasted with the part God plays. And, as Philippians 2:13 shows, even the part we have to play is possible only because He provides all that is necessary for the doing.

Something Luther Missed?

Let us get back to our phrase in Romans 1:17, "The just shall live by faith," and a significance of the words Luther may have missed.

The word here rendered *just* (it could also be translated *righteous*) is, according to Girdlestone, "almost always taken in the New Testament to represent that upright and merciful character [which is] in conformity with law."[7]

In Romans 1:17 Paul is quoting from Habakkuk 2:4. But it is interesting that there are many translations that in Habakkuk have the term *faithfulness,* or a variant, instead of *faith.* (Smith and Goodspeed, TEV, Moffatt, NEB, NASB, margin, etc.) Hence, we might read, "The just shall live by his faithfulness."

In agreement with this, *The New International Dictionary of New Testament Theology* informs us that the Hebrew term involved actually "means both faithfulness and faith," and " 'to show steadfastness in' and 'to believe in.' "[8]

In his commentary on Galatians, which has been hailed as among the finest ever written on the epistle, J. B. Lightfoot has an endnote on "The words denoting *Faith.*" In it he states that the Hebrew word, *emunah,* the Greek *pistis,* the Latin *fides,* and the English *faith,* "hover between two meanings; *trustfulness,* the frame of mind which relies on another; and *trustworthiness,* the frame of mind which can be relied upon." He further affirms that *trustfulness* and *trustworthiness* "are . . . connected together grammatically, . . . [and that] there is a close moral affinity between them."

He points out that we must have something of this double sense in Habakkuk 2:4.[9] *The New International Dictionary of New Testament Theology* concurs by observing that in the text *"Faithfulness* and *faith* stand here close together in the Hebrew term *[emunah.]"*[10]

This being so, we may see a pregnant double sense in Romans 1:17, one that brings together both justification, in the context of faith, and sanctification, in the context of faithfulness. And, surely, this has to be. As the Roman orator and statesman, Cicero, observed, "Where there is faith, there is also faithfulness." And, as we pointed out previously, John R. W. Stott maintains in connection with the Christian's personal relationship with Christ, that "it [is] impossible for us to think of justification as a purely external transaction."[11] Thus, to accept Girdlestone's explanation quoted above, we may understand our text, "The just shall live by faith," as meaning not only, (1) the just man does not live by relying on his own merits, but by his trust in Christ's merits, *but also,* (2) by faith he is able to *live* a life loyal to God because he trusts in Him to keep him faithful.

This idea is implied by the Amplified Bible's rendering, "The man who through faith is just *and* upright shall live *and* shall live by faith." [Italics in original.]

The same idea is intimated in Colossians 2:6: "As you have therefore received Christ Jesus the Lord [by faith], so walk [live day by day] in Him [by faith]."

The term *faithfulness* naturally connotes, among other things, a steadfast observance of God's requirements—obedience. Sanctification has loving obedience as its core.

To see Ellen White's perspective on the relationship between justification and sanctification in the above setting, it will be instructive to place two of her statements side by side. "The righteousness by which we are justified is imputed; the righteousness by which we are sanctified is imparted. The first is our title to heaven, the second is our fitness for heaven."[12] "Both our title to heaven [justification] and our fitness for it [sanctification] are found in the righteousness of Christ."[13] These words unmistakably make sanctification as well as justification a requisite for heaven.

And the terms "imputed" (inadequately but often defined as *credited* or *attributed*) and "imparted" *(actually given to someone so that it becomes his)* inform us neither of them are inherently ours, but are made ours by an outside source. Both are from God to us.

Let us take a further look at how sanctification as well as justification is contained in Romans 1:17. We may begin by looking at Romans chapters seven and eight. In chapter seven Paul describes the experience of an individual whose desire is to meet the demands of the moral law which he knows to be just and good. He strives to comply with those demands, but meets continual defeat because, although he is doing the best of which he is capable, he is trying in his own feeble strength. Through being continually worsted by his sinful nature and the machinations of Satan, he finally realizes he never can be victorious on his own, that he can never hope to receive the favor of God by his own marred efforts. He sees that "by the deeds of the law [trying to become acceptable to God by human effort] no flesh will be justified in His sight" (Romans 3:20). He begins to understand that, for the unregenerate, the law is a custodian to bring him to the only One who can reconcile him to God—Christ (Galatians 3:24). He understands that "a man is not justified by works of the law but by faith in Jesus Christ" (Galatians 2:16). So at last, with the light of the gospel finally beginning to illuminate his soul, and thus with a realization of the uselessness of his own efforts, he casts Himself in faith upon the mercy of God, grasps the promise that through Christ he is forgiven, and is cleansed and justified. So he exclaims, "I thank God—[I am delivered and justified]—through Jesus Christ our Lord" (Romans 7:25).

Faith is the vital ingredient in this experience. It is faith in Jesus' merits reckoned to himself that allows God to deliver him from sin and so accept him as though he had never sinned. This has to do with justification.

At this point in Romans eight, Paul moves to sanctification as a continuity with the experience of justification we dealt with in chapter nine of this book. Relieved of condemnation, walking "according to the Spirit," he states that now "the righteous requirement of the law" might "be fulfilled in" the Christian (Romans 8:4). This has to do with sanctification.

But take note that while the requirements of the law are now possible in the believer, it is not in his strength, but because by faith his mind and heart are "controlled by the Spirit" (verse 6). This is faithfulness by faith.

Are We Saved by Justification Alone?

The roles of justification and works in salvation need further examination. In the Bible the unacceptability of works is *always in the context of justification or grace*. Works can never be acceptable *for justification*. That can be ours only by God's grace.

But this does not eliminate works from salvation.

Let us emphasize again, we are not *justified* by works. But, as we have stated before, justification is not the only element connected with salvation. The idea that it is can become a bit of a red herring[14] which, drawn across our path, diverts our minds from the importance of works in salvation, and gives the idea that justification is all that is required for it.

John Wesley wrote that he had been unable to prove from Scripture that works have nothing to do with salvation.[15] Works are useless *for justification*. But the Word of Inspiration says, "All will be justified by their faith and judged by their works."[16] Here we have justification and works juxtaposed; both have a part in our salvation.

There are numerous Bible texts demonstrating that works are indeed connected with salvation. For example Paul, the great apostle of justification, writing of works, said that God "will render to each one according to his deeds," "glory, honor, and peace to everyone who works what is good, to the Jew first and also to the Greek" (Romans 2:6, 10). 1 Corinthians 9:24–27 qualifies as a discussion of necessary "works." Paul writes of "faith working" (Galatians 5:6). He tells us we are "created in Christ Jesus for good works" (Ephesians 2:10). (See also Psalm 62:12; Proverbs 24:12; Revelation 2:23; 20:12, 13.)

So the believer realizes that, even though he is now a justified child of God, certain "works," as an aspect of sanctification, are required and that he must have divine help to meet them. Then it is that he learns that the justified person finds sanctification as well as justification through Jesus. As *Today's English Version* puts it in 1 Corinthians 1:30, "God has brought you into union with Christ Jesus, and . . . by Him . . . we become God's holy [sanctified] people." "The just shall live [be sanctified] by faith."

The following statement stresses the relevance of works for the Christian. "The Word of God speaks to us as if everything depended upon our own efforts. We must come, we must resist the devil; we must strive to enter in at the strait gate; we must run the race with patience; we must fight the fight of faith; we must wrestle with principalities and powers; we must agonize before God in prayer, if we would stand blameless before the throne of God. We must have the faith that works, or it will be powerless. Good works will not pay the price of our redemption; they are the fruit of our faith in Jesus Christ, who is our righteousness."[17]

Justification and Sanctification Inseparable

We have shown in chapter nine that justification has both its objective and subjective consequences. Objectively, the repentant sinner in faith turns his eyes to Christ and so is accepted by God with Jesus' righteousness credited to him. But simultaneously he is born again, which is a subjective experience. And one part is of a piece with the other. As hydrogen cannot be separated from oxygen and you still have water, neither can you separate the subjective experience of justification from the objective, and still have justification.

Note how the following quotation highlights the difference between the religious efforts of the unregenerate and the regenerate: "All that [the unregenerate] man can do without Christ is polluted with selfishness and sin; but that which is wrought through faith [by the regenerate] is acceptable to God."[18]

"To oppose faith to works," wrote A. W. Tozer, "is to make the fruit the enemy of the tree; yet that is exactly what we have managed to do."[19]

Objectively, when the sinner, in acknowledged, abject soul poverty and helplessness, turns to Christ *in penitence,* submission, and faith, he is pardoned, and Christ's merits, perfect obedience, and sacrifice for sin, are placed to his account as his very own. The sinner has nothing with which to pay for this. It must come as a totally free gift, or he can never acquire it. It is a gift lavishly offered by God. The condition for receiving it, we repeat, is penitence, submission, and faith. "The unconditional pardon of sin never has been, and never will be."[20] Justification being accomplished, the emphasis turns to *living.* The person who has been justified will live a certain quality of life. That is the life that is possible as one receives the life of Christ as his own. This is the life Paul is writing about. "It is no longer I who live," he pens, "but Christ lives in me, and the life which I now live in the flesh I live *by faith* in the Son of God" (Galatians 2:20).

There you have it! The just shall live by faith in what Jesus can do for and in him—as he faithfully cooperates with Jesus. Thus he lives—

The Life of Faith

The life of faith is an attitude of constantly looking to Jesus alone in all things, not depending on our own resources, talents, and strengths for living the Christian life. It becomes an automatic impulse to turn to Him in every situation, not slavishly, but lovingly, trustingly, as a little child looks to his father for wisdom and strength he does not himself possess.

The life of faith is trusting God in the darkness as well as in the light, affirming like Job, "Though He slay me, yet will I trust in Him."

The life of faith is a life of restfulness, knowing that the present and future are in the infinitely capable hands of One who knows, and is in control of all things, Who is very deeply interested in us, and Who "doeth all things well."

The life of faith unto salvation is one in which we are required to work. In the present context the work we refer to is not that of laboring for or witnessing to others, essential though that be. It is the work we are required to do, in cooperation with God, to shape our own lives and characters for heaven. It is being employed in the pursuit of holiness. "Pursue ... holiness, without which no one will see the Lord" (Hebrews 12:14). Holiness, as we have pointed out, is a synonym for sanctification, which is a process by which we day by day strive in His strength to reflect His character more and more. "The followers of Christ are to become like Him—by the grace of God to form characters in harmony with the principles of His holy law. This is Bible sanctification."[21]

The life of faith is a life of victory over sin. "This is the victory that has overcome the world—our faith" (1 John 5:4). This victory comes, not because of the victorious *person* but because of the victorious *power*. The Christian is connected to divine power that he may have unbroken victory.

"The New Covenant provides a guarantee, not only for God's faithfulness, *but for man's too.*"[22] [Italics supplied.]

We conclude, then, that it cannot be insisted that justification is more important than sanctification because justification is by faith and sanctification is not. Both are by faith. Nor can we insist that justification stands supremely alone in salvation, but that sanctification is virtually optional. We remind ourselves once more that justification is our title to heaven, and sanctification is our fitness for heaven. Neither is optional.

Finally, we remind ourselves that the goal of the gospel is sanctification (1 Thessalonians 4:3), that it is the inevitable fruit of justification.

1. Page 676.
2. Volume 6, page 880.
3. Taylor, Richard S., *Exploring Christian Holiness*, (Kansas City, MO: Beacon Hill Press of Kansas City, ©1985), Volume 2, pages 151, 152.
4. White, *Testimonies for the Church*, Volume 6, page 426.
5. White, *Review and Herald*, November 29, 1892.
6. White, *Manuscript Releases*, Volume 4, page 113, 114.

7. Girdlestone, Robert Baker, *Synonyms of the Old Testament,* (Grand Rapids, MI: William B. Eerdmans Publishing Company, ©1974), page 168.
8. Brown, Colin, editor, *The New International Dictionary of New Testament Theology,* (Grand Rapids, MI: Zondervan Publishing House, ©1978), Volume 3, page 368.
9. Lightfoot, J. B., *St. Paul's Epistle to the Galatians,* (Lynn, MA: Hendrickson Publishers, Inc., ©1982), pages 154, 155.
10. Brown, Loc. Cit.
11. Stott, Op. Cit., page 191.
12. White, *The Faith I Live By,* page 116.
13. White, *The Desire of Ages,* page 300.
14. This figure comes from British fox hunting. Opponents of the pastime might drag a red herring across the path of the hounds hoping they will follow that odor rather than that of the fox.
15. Wynkoop, Op. Cit., page 212.
16. White, *Testimonies for the Church,* Volume 4, page 386.
17. White, *Address to Ministers,* page 7.
18. White, *Faith and Works,* page 94.
19. Tozer, A. W., *A Treasury of A. W. Tozer,* page 156.
20. White, *God's Amazing Grace,* page 73.
21. White, *The Great Controversy,* page 469.
22. *The Treasury of Andrew Murray,* (Grands Rapids, MI: Baker Book House, ©1969), page 1658.

Chapter 13
God's Part:
Providing the Way of Escape

*P*eople who are preparing to receive the latter rain are, when tempted, presented a way of escape which, if understood and followed, will greatly simplify their battle with temptation.

Under existing circumstances, God has made life as simple for us as He can. (We ourselves are often responsible for the tangles we get into.) The frustrating complexities of our world are a result of sin. How simple life would be if for every problem that confronted us we needed only one answer, a kind of universal solvent which would dissolve every difficulty. Of course life is much, much too complicated for that. And yet . . . !

1 Corinthians 10:13 is a familiar and heartening text to many Christians when harassed by strong and persistent temptations. "No temptation has overtaken you that is not common to man. God is faithful, and He will not let you be tempted beyond your strength, but with the temptation will also provide the way of escape, that you may be able to endure it" (RSV).

Reading that, you probably caught the word *the*—*the* way of escape—where other translations have "*a* way of escape." But *the* is correct, according to the Greek.

However, *a way* is acceptable. In exegeting this text the *Tyndale New Testament Commentaries* notes that the language suggests a narrow mountain defile in which an army is trapped with seemingly no way out. But God is never at a loss; He has the particular way of escape for His child in every situation. In fact, "Our heavenly Father has a thousand ways to provide for us, of which we know nothing."[1]

God provides for you and me the one primary way of escape which, if we take that way, makes it so much easier for Him to open another one needed in a particular situation. That one way is like the only door out of a room in which we are shut up. But when we use the key and get through that door, we enter another room that has a thousand exits. So when we take the one door God wants us to take, that makes it possible for Him to open for us any one of a thousand possible doors. To understand this point, we need to switch to another subject temporarily.

The Matrix of Sin

The central sin of humanity is that of selfishness. Man's greatest idol is self. In our natural state we are locked into that room of selfishness. We were born in that room. We were born selfish. All other sins we commit in one way or another are connected with and spring from that matrix.

So we may say that every form in which sin manifests itself to us is selfishness, even though that selfishness be disguised in a thousand different garbs, sometimes apparently innocent or virtuous-appearing. In fact, much religious activity is based on selfishness. As A. W. Tozer wrote, "How much eager-beaver religious work is done out of a carnal desire to make good? How many hours of prayer are wasted beseeching God to bless projects that are geared to the glorification of little men? How much sacred money is poured out upon men who, in spite of their tear-in-voice appeals, nevertheless seek only to make a fair show of the flesh?"[2]

So we become irritable because self is "rubbed the wrong way." We manifest a quick temper because in some manner self has been crossed. We are envious or jealous because we grudgingly perceive someone else as being something, or possessing something, superior to what we are or have, so self resents him for that.

Often we are critical of someone else because there is a secret, selfish jealousy of that person. We become self-defensive because pride has been offended. Self erects a barrier of pride around itself to protect its dignity, thus it insulates itself from admitting wrong, and so shuts us off from repentance.

All lust is selfish. Lust sometimes even destroys others to gratify self. The love of pleasure is selfish. All dishonesty is selfishness. Covetousness is the selfishness which desires for self things that belong to others.

We manifest contempt for another because pride has caused us to overvalue ourselves. We denigrate another with the hope it will elevate ourselves. We are arrogant because we perceive ourselves as superior to others. We lie because we want to shelter self. We become unreasonable—and we know we are—because in some way we are driven to shield self. Self-right-eousness, self-defense, self-satisfaction, self-sufficiency, self-gratification, self-worship, self-assertiveness. When does the catalog stop?

Satan, then, invariably tempts us on the basis of some point of selfishness. It was by appealing to Adam and Eve on that basis that he managed to overcome them (because of Adam's disobedience "a discordant element, born of selfishness, entered man's life"[3]); and it is by appealing to some aspect of this potential, many-faceted selfishness that he baits us. This is his universal channel to the human heart.

God's Way of Closing the Channel

If selfishness, the central sin, is Satan's universal channel to tempt and overcome us, logic and common sense tell us closing off that channel involves dealing with selfishness.

At this point let's examine another Bible text—James 4:7, "Therefore submit to God. Resist the devil and he will flee from you." The KJV makes it more emphatic: "Submit *yourselves* therefore to God. Resist the devil and he will flee from you." [Italics supplied.] I propose that *in this text God has given us a clue to that one basic solution which provides a resolution for all our sin problems;* there is in it a universal sin "resolvent." This primary solution is a simple one. We all know it in theory. It is the submission, the surrender of ourselves and all that self embraces, to God.

When we yield ourselves—*our self, our ego*—to God, we sweep aside the dominant impediment to God doing everything He wishes for us. Unless we do this we retain in our own hearts, upon the throne of our lives where God must take His seat, the enemy which makes it impossible for Him to take the central place in our lives. That throne is wide enough for only one. Besides, God will never share us with anyone or anything else.

So, God's way of escape is made possible by our submitting ourselves—every aspect of self—to Him. When we do this, we make it possible for Him to rescue us from the devil, to throw up a wall between us and the enemy, and to empower us to defeat him. Until we do surrender, God's hands are more or less tied.

> Jesus gained the victory through submission and faith in God, and by the apostle He says to us, "Submit yourselves therefore to God. Resist the devil, and he will flee from you. Draw nigh to God, and He will draw nigh to you." James 4:7, 8. We cannot

save ourselves from the tempter's power; he has conquered humanity, and when we try to stand in our own strength, we shall become a prey to his devices; but "the name of the Lord is a strong tower: the righteous runneth into it, and is safe." Prov. 18:10. Satan trembles and flees before the weakest soul who finds refuge in that mighty name.[4]

1. White, *The Desire of Ages,* page 330.
2. *The Best of A. W. Tozer,* (Grand Rapids, MI: Baker Book House, ©1978), pages 47, 48.
3. White, *Signs of the Times,* June 13, 1900.
4. White, *The Desire of Ages,* pages 130, 131.

Chapter 14
Our Part:
Taking His Way

*T*he people who receive the latter rain will have surrendered fully, unequivocally, to Jesus. By thus placing themselves unreservedly in His hands and thrusting self out of the way, they will have made it possible for Him to give them continual victory over temptation and sin.

Over the years I have asked a question of many Seventh-day Adventist audiences, the response to which has been quite revealing to me.

I have started by beginning to quote the second part of the text we began to discuss in the previous chapter, "Resist . . . ." And the audience has had no problem finishing—". . . the devil and he will flee from you."

Then I have asked, "What does the first part of the text say?" Almost invariably only one or two in the audience will have the answer. But, as we have seen, *the first part of the text is by far the most important.*

"Submit yourselves [self] . . . to God" (James 4:7, KJV).

There is very little point in resisting the devil, or in battling self, if we do not first surrender self and the will to God. If we try to overcome the blandishments or pressures of the flesh, the devil, or the world without having yielded to God, we are resisting in our own strength, not God's. When we do that, we are defeated before we begin.

Unregenerate humanity is rebellious by nature, and generally does not want to and cannot, correct itself. And when there is a momentary impulse to overcome a failing in the life, it is a case of self pitted against self, a house divided against itself, which cannot stand (Mark 3:25). In this instance it cannot stand against Satan.

> Without Christ he [the Christian] is unable to subdue a single sin or overcome the smallest temptation.[1]

Jesus gained the victory through submission and faith in God, and by the apostle He says to us, "Submit yourselves therefore to God. Resist the devil, and he will flee from you. Draw nigh to God, and He will draw nigh to you." James 4:7, 8. We cannot save ourselves from the tempter's power; he has conquered humanity, and when we try to stand in our own strength, we shall become a prey to his devices.[2]

Meeting Sudden, Surprise Temptations

In the daily life you will meet with sudden surprises, disappointments, and temptations. What saith the word? "Resist the devil," by firm reliance upon God, "and he will flee from you. Draw nigh to God, and He will draw nigh to you." "Let him take hold of My strength, that he may make peace with Me; and he shall make peace with Me." Look unto Jesus at all times and in all places, offering a silent prayer from a sincere heart that you may know how to do His will. Then when the enemy comes in like a flood, the Spirit of the Lord will lift up a standard for you against the enemy.[3]

When I have asked my audiences to repeat the first part of James 4:7, the response, or lack of response, could lead to the conclusion that, in our Christianity, many of us are fighting our battles against Satan and sin to a large degree with our own resources, without recognizing the uselessness of that exercise.

Before we ponder this further, there are a few things we should note.

Submit is in a tense in the Greek which conveys, "No indecisiveness, no wobbling. Yield right now!" When we realize temptation and its danger, and recognize that in our weakness we are in jeopardy, hesitation in turning to God and asking Him for help can be dangerous. Satan sees our wavering and presses in to take the advantage.

Christ taught us an invaluable lesson regarding dealing with temptation. In a description of Satan's enticement of Jesus on the Mount of Temptation, offering to deliver the world to Christ if He would pay homage to Satan, we read, "The eyes of Jesus rested for a moment upon the scene before him; he then turned resolutely from it, refusing to dally with the tempter by even looking upon the enchanting prospect he had presented to him."[4]

As Jesus turned away from the temptation the moment He realized what it was, so must we.

The same emphasis applies to *resist* as to *submit*. Having surrendered to God, we are then *immediately* to resolutely, firmly oppose Satan—in the strength God gives us, which strength is still not our own. "I can of mine own self do nothing" (John 5:30, KJV). When we so resist in Christ's strength, Satan recognizes he is a defeated foe.

Victory Is Not Postponed Until Tomorrow

When we submit ourselves, our egos, to Jesus He gives us the victory over every sin, right now. But the war is not thereby over. We must hour by hour, day by day, meet and in His strength, overcome the *temptations* that pour in upon us from the world, the flesh, and the devil. The Christian's battle, then, is actually not to be with sin but with *temptation*.

A problem we have is that when we read about overcoming, we understand overcoming *sin*. We understand it this way because the terminology is not always precise so that the language sometimes leads to that understanding.

What the Christian must overcome is the *temptation* to sin, which is implied in the phrasing but not generally deduced. If he overcomes the temptation to commit a particular sin, he obviously does not sin.

> Temptations will pour in upon us, for by them we are to be tried during our probation upon earth. This is the proving of God, a revelation of our own hearts. There is no sin in having temptations; but sin comes in when temptation is yielded to.[5]

The Epistle of James clears up this point. "Each person is tempted when he is lured and enticed by his own desire. Then desire when it has conceived gives birth to sin" (James 1:14, 15, RSV).

Some aspect of our fallen natures, some appetite or passion, sensibility or impulse, is a channel to entice us to do something wrong.

We may illustrate it by thinking about fishing. Let's suppose that sin is a fisherman, the bait on his hook is some temptation, and you and I are the fish.

The fisherman dangles the appetizing bait in front of us alluringly. Our attention is attracted, and thus we are tempted. But that is not sin. Now we must decide what we are going to do about that bait, that temptation. We have to make some decisions. Right here judgment and will become involved, and must deal with the desire that has been created by the bait.

Kinds of Temptations

Temptations are of two kinds, although these may overlap. First, there are temptations from external sources that the human heart may find alluring, pleasant, desirable. I label this broad category, temptations of the world.

The second kind is internal, having to do with attitudes. These find their origin in the heart. In this category are inducements to become irritable, angry, resentful, jealous, vain, bitter, faultfinding, and such. I term these, temptations of the spirit.

The Christian who maintains a relationship with Christ will probably be bothered only marginally by the first kind. The temptations to sin he faces far more, and which to him are much more dangerous, are of the second category—the spiritual.

The Christian does not want to be angry, or irritable, or bitter. He knows these emotions are wrong. But he is faced with situations that tempt him to these, much more often than to those that may be called worldly. And they may be stirred in such ways that they may seem to be justifiable, or at least excusable. For instance, a child may be balky, so inciting irritation or anger. Now, you want to train your child right. You have an obligation to do so. But by being balky he is challenging your authority, which tends to arouse irritation. So you are prompted to protect your authority, which is proper, but you are tempted to do so in anger, with more physical force than you should.

Scenarios might be suggested in the marriage, in the work place, in the church, in any area in which situations arise which imply the desirable and perceived necessity to protect rights, and in which the Christian is strongly tempted to have resentment, impatience, irritation, jealousy, and so on. Each such impulse is, in one way or another, a desire to vindicate or protect self.

In giving way to these impulses, these temptations, we have taken sin's bait, and have sinned.

The whole process, then, as we have said, is primarily in handling *temptation*. This temptation appeals to some weakness of ours, and a desire is implanted in the mind and emotions to respond. But *not until* we respond to the desire and allow the bait to pull us, have we sinned. Sin *begins* when we yield to the temptation, even if only in our minds (See Matthew 5:27–30). We may never actually act on it because of foreseen repercussions. But, having even mentally accepted the bait, we are involved with sin, for it is at that point the fisherman, Sin, has hooked us.

So the great battle we must win is on the level of temptation. When we recognize that a certain course we are tempted to follow leads to sin, that recognition ought to be all that is necessary to cause us immediately to turn from it. That was all that was necessary for Jesus to turn from it.

So why do we sometimes hesitate? Because our wills are not yet, not at the moment, not really, set against the sin? Because we play, even though briefly, with a perversity in the heart which wants what the temptation offers?

A major—*the* major—reason why Christians have so many problems with temptation is because they equivocate, hesitate, play with doubts, consult their carnal desires, weigh the losses and gains. Too often there is the progression described by Augustine: "A thought, a picture, a fascination, a fall."

I have stated that when we submit ourselves to Jesus, He *immediately* makes victory, ongoing victory over temptation and sin, possible for us. We will have battles to fight after surrender, many of them. But if we maintain our submission, we fight not sin but temptation. Consequently, *we will not sin* if through Christ we continually gain the victory *over temptation.*

Wrestling With Sin or Battling Temptation?

Some may not clearly see the difference between wrestling with sin and battling temptation. There is a vital difference, although it is not always well understood.

It is the difference between a soldier, anxious to battle the foe yet encumbered with his foe's (sin's) chains and trying to fight with a broken sword; and a soldier who is free, unfettered, and fully equipped for battle.

It is the difference between a small boy confronted by a bully (sin) and unable to adequately take care of himself, and a big brother (Jesus) standing beside him who is larger and stronger than the bully.

It is the difference between the shorn Samson helpless to overcome his enemies, and Samson true to his vow and endowed with strength that was supernatural.

It is the difference between an adversary superior to you (sin) being inside your house (heart), dominating you, harassing you, goading you, so that you are not the master of your house, while the One who can help you (Jesus) is locked outside so that He cannot aid; and your Deliverer being inside with you, having expelled the enemy, making you the master of your own house, while it is the enemy who is outside, persistently trying to get in, yes, but nevertheless outside.

In the first case, the householder cannot help being dominated, played with, manipulated. In the second case, while he must be constantly alert, he is free to do as he wishes.

> "He who is in you is greater than he who is in the world" (1 John 4:4).

But many Christians use their wills alone to wrestle with sin or temptation rather than to surrender the situation to Jesus and accept His victory, instead of trying to accomplish their own. So they fight, and wrestle, and struggle, and never really get the victory, even though they may make some progress. And the battle goes on day after day, month after month, year after year, most of the time ending in defeat. And they wonder, "The Bible tells me only the overcomer will sit with Jesus on His throne. When will I finally have the victory over my sins so that I shall be an overcomer?" It is essential that we recognize that the carnal heart, the unregenerate will, has not the ability to deal with sin and temptation on its own.

What is Surrender?

This surrender is our response to God's drawing, so that He can shatter all our inner resistance to His will, change our minds, radically rechannel our attitudes, motives, desires—the whole heart—so that our selfish "rights" are abandoned, and His will continually sought. It is a supernatural experience that is possible only at the foot of the cross. In this surrender we recognize God's claims upon every facet of our lives, and give Him the right to expect us to conform to His pattern for us.

"To have the religion of Christ means that you have absolutely surrendered your all to God, and consented to the guidance of the Holy Spirit."[6]

Think of the results of such a total submission.

When we submit to God, we give up depending on our own strength which is but weakness, our own pride which inclines us to muddle through even though we know we are doing miserably. It casts aside the hindrances of our own self-seeking, our own "wisdom" which is but foolishness.

When we submit to God, we remove that self-sufficiency, that independence, that which makes it impossible for Him to do what He knows needs to be done.

A woman and I stood at the bottom of the stairs and talked while a number of other guests said goodnight. She was about thirty-five, and we had not conversed for long before I began to realize that she was experiencing a deep spiritual hunger. She had not been inside a Seventh-day Adventist church in four years, she told me, since her husband had had a bitter experience with some leaders.

We talked about barriers that sometimes stand between Jesus and us. We spoke of how, by surrendering to Him, we may get rid of bitterness and live a victorious life.

Suddenly, she exclaimed, tears glistening in her eyes, "I want to surrender to Jesus, right now!"

So we bowed our heads together and prayed. And the commitment was made. She had responded to the drawing of Jesus. There was no resistance—only joyous surrender.

1. White, *Signs of the Times,* January 24, 1878.
2. White, *The Desire of Ages,* pages 130, 131.
3. White, *The Adventist Home,* page 24.
4. White, *The Spirit of Prophecy,* Volume 2, page 96.
5. White, *Testimonies for the Church,* Volume 4, page 358.
6. White, *Messages to Young People,* page 30.

PART THREE

Chapter 15
But What If I Fail?

Some new Christians almost seem to be programmed or conditioned to take it for granted that they are going to fail. They factor failure into their equation for Christian living. And sure enough, they fail, they sin. And some older Christians have found themselves failing and failing so frequently they have arrived at the place where they virtually consider it *normal*.

When getting into a subject like this it's easy to be misunderstood. Especially at this point I desire not to be misunderstood. So please follow me carefully.

"So you believe in sinless perfection?" some will accuse at this juncture. Or, "So you expect to be walking around like little Jesuses!" Or, "You think that a Christian is not supposed to make mistakes?"

I am all too well aware that Christians make mistakes, that they sometimes sin. I am aware of this from painful personal experience. And "sins . . . overcame Noah, Lot, Moses, Abraham, David, and Solomon, and . . . even Elijah's strong spirit sank under temptation during his fearful trial. Jonah's disobedience and Israel's idolatry are faithfully recorded. Peter's denial of Christ, the sharp contention of Paul and Barnabas, the failings and infirmities of the prophets and apostles, are all laid bare by the Holy Ghost, who lifts the veil from the human heart."[1]

Now, because those illustrious men sinned, it is easy for us to use their failures as an excuse for our sins. But this we must not do. "There is no excuse for sin,"[2] neither theirs nor anyone else's.

Still, John, recognizing the possibility of Christians sinning, wrote, "If anyone sins, we have an Advocate with the Father, Jesus Christ the righteous" (1 John 2:1).

But before he penned those words he wrote, "My children, in writing thus to you my purpose is that you should not commit sin" (verse 1, NEB). There are a couple things we may note about the Greek of this text. First, the Greek tense tells us that John's desire is that on no occasion would his Christian readers sin. Says J. Howard Marshall in exegeting this text, John's aim "was that Christians should not sin," that they "would recognize the all-pervasive character of sin—yet not sin."[3] Writing of the same text, Raymond E. Brown insists "that more is meant here than an urging not to be an habitual sinner (so that occasional sins would be tolerable)—the author is placing upon the Johannine Christian the same . . . demand that Jesus placed on the healed paralytic: 'Sin no more.' John 5:14."[4]

Second, as we have seen, "sin not" means not one single act of sin. So John's wish for his readers is that they at no time commit even one sin.

John Emphasizes Not Sinning

John's emphasis, then, is not on the Christian sinning, but on his not sinning. And this is stressed throughout this epistle. See, for example, 1 John 3:6, 9; 5:4, 18.

Nowadays our thinking is inclined to be the opposite: We can hardly conceive the idea of weak, flawed, fallible human beings not committing sin. Anyone supposing it possible has to be a fanatic, or a religious enthusiast who is out of touch with reality; or someone who does not understand the deep, black, sinfulness of the human heart. In our weakness—and may we also say, lack of faith—we may consider the concept of sin-no-more as incredible.

But we must let the Word speak for itself, and not stumble over it because it may not correspond with our theology, or our experience. And we must remember that we are to look, not at man's weakness and state of sinfulness—that is not the criterion—but at God's strength.

If it is not possible for you and me always to overcome sin, John himself was a religious enthusiast, or a fanatic, or out of touch. He is indicted by his own words quoted above. Ellen White was the same. For she wrote, by way of illustration, "Exact obedience is required, and those who say that it is not possible to live a perfect life throw upon God the imputation of injustice and untruth."[5]

"He who has not sufficient faith in Christ to believe that he can keep him from sinning, has not the faith that will give him an entrance into the kingdom of God."[6]

The thrust of all of this is unmistakable.

You and I, then, are not to submit to the hazily-sensed, negative, mental reservation that we are probably going to sin a bit every day. Instead we are to look constantly in faith to Him "who is able to keep [us] from stumbling" (Jude 24). For He is continually able, moment by moment, to keep us from falling into sin.

(At this stage we should perhaps briefly review what we concluded about sin and temptation in the previous chapter. You recall we pointed out that the Christian is not primarily called to deal with sin but with temptation. By the grace and power of God we may overcome *temptation*—all the time (See 1 Corinthians 10:13; Ephesians 6:13; 2 Peter 2:9; Jude 24). But if through Jesus we overcome temptation all the time, we are avoiding sinning all the time, because sinning is giving in to, being overcome by, temptation (James 1:14, 15). It seems to me that most serious Seventh-day Adventists will agree on this.

But What About When We Fail?

But what about when we do fail, as we recognize we sometimes do? What do we do about a "surprise sin," when we momentarily give way to a sudden, strong, temptation? This, we would think, is what John had in mind when he wrote 1 John 2:1.

Or what do we do when discouragement overtakes us and we fail? Or when we become tired, so our spiritual arm grows weary and our shield of faith sags?

We shall take up this question in the following chapter. Meanwhile, I want to stress some things we should not do.

Don't Do These Things

Whatever may have been the reason for your falling—

➤ Don't, when almost overwhelmed with a sense of guilt because you failed, tell yourself that God will not forgive and cleanse you. Remember that Christ is your Advocate and your High Priest, and that if you go to Him in true contrition, He will take your case.

➤ Don't decide, I'm hopeless. Christianity isn't for me so it's no use. I might as well quit.

➤ Don't be tempted to despair because Satan suggests your sins are too great for forgiveness. Remember, Christ has been made sin for you, and no sin is too great for Him to forgive if we confess sincerely.

➤ Don't accept Satan's suggestion that you have committed the unpardonable sin.

➤ Don't, because you feel your weakness and vulnerability, and think of the subtlety and strength of the adversary, be tempted to sink down in helplessness. Remember, Christ is your "strong tower," your "munitions of rocks," your "hiding place."

➤ Don't allow discouragement or depression to take over. There is a text that every Christian should memorize: Isaiah 50:10. It starts off like this: "Who among you fears the Lord? Who obeys the voice of His servant?" So this is for anyone who genuinely trusts and serves God. And yet at times he or she "walks in darkness and has no light." Discouragement, doubt, despondency, may envelop him or her. At such times, "Let him trust in the name of the Lord and rely upon his God."

➤ Don't harbor the idea that God has tuned you out.

➤ Don't decide, "People know I've failed and I'm too embarrassed to go back to church anymore. So I'm not going back."

➤ Don't excuse or justify yourself, putting the blame on some other person, God, or circumstances.

➤ Don't conclude that because you have failed God is unjust, expecting something you cannot produce. Sin in its deceitfulness is always endeavoring to persuade us that the requirements of God's law are unfair, or unjust, or indeed impossible.

➤ Don't decide, "Well, I've tried hard but haven't succeeded. That proves that no one can really meet God's requirements, so I'm just going to stop trying so hard and just accept that Jesus loves me anyway and my obedience or disobedience are not that important." The fact is, there is no place in Scripture that tells us we sin because we cannot help it, and therefore can excuse ourselves.

➤ Don't, because you know that in you, in your flesh, dwells no good thing, think you can never be delivered from "this body of death." This phrase, I suggest, means the body and its faculties whose appetites and passions, impulses and sensibilities, are gone awry, weakened and perverted, and are consequently manipulated and misused by sin to the frustration and discouragement of one who has not yet learned the secret of conquering through Jesus. But *you can overcome.* "We can overcome. Yes; fully, entirely. Jesus died to make a way of escape for us, that we might overcome every evil temper, every sin, every temptation, and sit down at last with Him."[7]

➤ Don't think your case hopeless because you glimpse something of the great holiness of God and His abhorrence of sin, and then become sensible of your own sinfulness. Remember, Christ is your righteousness. When you are in Him, the Father sees you as He sees His Son.

➤ Don't be intimidated when temptations press on every side. Christ is the Good Shepherd who keeps unsleeping watch over His sheep, and allows nothing to come to them but that which is ultimately for their good.

There is a very important question that is often asked in connection with our falling into sin, that we must look at. Are we rejected of God when we sin?

Are We Rejected When We Sin?

There is some misunderstanding among not a few Seventh-day Adventists as to our relationship with God when we sin. There is, for example, the understanding that our falling into sin does nothing to our justification—that we are still justified. In proof of this *Steps to Christ,* page 64, is read: "Even if we are overcome by the enemy, we are not cast off, not forsaken and rejected of God. No; Christ is at the right hand of God, who also maketh intercession for us."

According to this quotation we have been "overcome," which means we have sinned. But the fact that we are "not cast off, not forsaken and rejected," it is said, demonstrates we are still in a state of justification.

But notice what is written further along in the same paragraph, referring to those who have been overcome. God "desires to *restore* you to Himself. . . . And if you will but *yield* yourself to Him, He that hath begun a good work in you will carry it forward to the day of Jesus Christ." [Italics supplied.]

To be restored means to be returned to a former place or condition. Obviously, then, by sinning we have fallen from a position which is involved with our salvation.

Observe the following: "All are fallible, all make mistakes and fall into sin; but if the wrongdoer is willing to see his errors, as they are made plain by the convicting Spirit of God, and in humility of heart will confess them, . . . *then he may be restored.*"[8] [Italics supplied.]

One more helpful quote: "If through manifold temptations we are surprised or deceived into sin, He does not turn from us and leave us to perish."[9] No, He labors to restore us—*but we must be restored!*

131

"While God can be just, and yet justify the sinner through the merits of Christ, no man can cover his soul with the garments of Christ's righteousness while practicing known sins, or neglecting known duties. God requires the entire surrender of the heart, before justification can take place; and in order for man to retain justification, there must be continual obedience, through active, living faith that works by love and purifies the soul."[10]

1. White, *Testimonies for the Church,* Volume 4, page 12.
2. White, *Review and Herald,* September 24, 1901.
3. Marshall, J. Howard, *The New International Commentary on the New Testament,* "The Epistles of John," (Grand Rapids, MI: William B. Eerdmans Publishing Company, ©1990), page 116.
4. Brown, Raymond E., "The Epistles of John," *The Anchor Bible,* (New York, NY: Doubleday, ©1982), Volume 30, page 215. Edited by William F. Albright and David Noel Freedman.
5. White, *Review and Herald,* February 7, 1857.
6. White, *Review and Herald,* March 10, 1904.
7. White, *Testimonies for the Church,* Volume 1, page 144.
8. White, *That I May Know Him,* page 238.
9. White, *Seventh-day Adventist Bible Commentary,* Volume 7, page 984.
10. White, *Selected Messages,* Book 1, page 366.

Chapter 16
Our Part:
Turn Back

The Christian may have a sense of security and stability, but only in Christ, never in Himself. It is found only in Christ because on Christ's part the connection is eternal, unbreakable. But it is fragile, brittle on our part, because we are fragile, brittle, fallible. Thus, while we must have "no confidence in the flesh" (Philippians 3:3), "the mountains shall depart and the hills be removed, but my kindness shall not depart from you, nor shall my covenant of peace be removed, says the Lord who has mercy on you" (Isaiah 54:10).

So, as we discussed in the previous chapter, in his or her weakness and fallibility, a true Christian may sometimes fail and sin. But he or she is not thereby rejected. However, he or she does need to be restored.

But when we do sin, what must we do to be restored?

Don't Waste Time

When you and I realize we have sinned, let us allow no time to elapse in making things right. "Let him [immediately] take hold of My strength, that he may make peace with Me; and he shall make peace with Me" (Isaiah 27:5).

There are a number of reasons why, when we have sinned we must waste no time in turning resolutely to our Savior in penitence, confession and renunciation of sin. First, life is always fragile and uncertain. While God gives "ample opportunity for repentance,"[1] and "is very patient with you, because it is not His will for any to be lost, but for all to come to repentance" (2 Peter 3:9, NEB), we never really know what even the next few moments have in store for us.

Secondly, the longer we neglect returning, the harder it usually becomes. The urgency and the feeling of the necessity to confess fade, and the sin begins to appear less heinous. We might even conclude that, really, it was not so serious that we need bother ourselves about it.

Moreover, as we put off confession, pride and ego begin to make large the humiliation of admitting we were wrong. Stubbornness may harden the heart, and there may even be a growth of resentment at being required to humiliate self by confession. To that extent one sin allowed to linger in the heart will eventually affect even the most genuine Christian.

A further reason for immediate confession is that if we persist in delaying or refusing to confess, a change in attitude toward God and His will develops. Whereas before, in the real Christian, there was an eager willingness to obey God, a discord now begins to develop between Him and us. We must not push aside this possibility as being a fantasy. The peril growing from such a situation is expressed in these words: "It is not the greatness of the act of disobedience that constitutes sin, but the fact of variance from God's expressed will in the least particular; for this shows that there is yet communion between the soul and sin. The heart is divided in its service."[2]

There is one more hazard we want to draw attention to. We have discussed, in chapter nine, a dangerous notion accepted by some, which tends to mitigate the urgency of making our sins right as soon as we are convicted of them. This is the subtle idea that a sin (or at least certain kinds of sins) does not affect our justification. If this is so, why the rush? one might rationalize. If it is justification alone that makes our salvation possible, and we can retain justification with sin in the life, why do we need to make the sin right? Especially if it means having to humiliate self and confess and perhaps make restitution to someone else? Under the logic of this sort of reasoning one might postpone, or fail altogether, to confess what he or she knows is a sin.

The fact is, of course, that one known, unconfessed sin, or breaching of the "royal law" (James 2:8), brings down upon us the condemning weight and the objective guilt of the whole law, as the closing quotation of the previous chapter insists.

"For whosoever shall keep the whole law, and yet offend in one point, he is guilty of all" (James 2:10, KJV). As *The New International Dictionary of New Testament Theology* has it, "Every single sin, however insignificant it may appear to be, makes the doer 'totally guilty,' and therefore liable to judgment."[3]

"The little sins that men think are of so trivial a character that on their account they will not be brought into condemnation, are very offensive in the sight of God."[4]

But we do not need to become entangled in situations such as the above.

"Come ... Just As You Are"

> Whatever may have been your past experience, however discouraging your present circumstances, if you will come to Jesus just as you are, weak, helpless, and despairing, our compassionate Saviour will meet you a great way off, and will throw about you His arms of love and His robe of righteousness. He presents us to the Father clothed in the white raiment of His own character.[5]

In chapters seven and eight we discussed repentance and conversion. We have come to these subjects again in this chapter, but only to remind ourselves that when we stumble and sin, and desire to make it right with God, we are led through essentially the same steps we took when we were born again. Because, as we have seen, we need to be restored. The process may take only minutes, but a little reflection will show us that we do retrace those steps.

Let's illustrate by supposing that something caused me to speak a sharp word to my wife. God convicts me that I have sinned, and at the same time in love He tries to draw me back toward Himself. I respond to that constraint and conviction; I do not resist.

He then makes me sorry for failing Him, and I confess that I have let Him down, and I make things right with my wife.

Now that I have truly and sincerely confessed, God can constantly and unhesitatingly forgive and cleanse me of the sin that has, to whatever degree, come between Him and me. I must then believe and accept the fact that He has forgiven and cleansed me of that repudiated and confessed sin. He then empowers me so that I need not fail again, and He lives in me by His Spirit.

With the Holy Spirit within, I am to bring forth much fruit (John 15:5), the fruits of the Spirit, "love, joy, peace, longsuffering, kindness, goodness, faithfulness, gentleness, self-control" (Galatians 5:22, 23).

"For every class of temptations there is a remedy. We are not left to ourselves to fight the battle against self and our sinful natures in our own finite strength. Jesus is a mighty helper, a never-failing support. . . . None need fail or become discouraged, when such ample provision has been made for us."[6]

We have come now to the end of our study. We have examined the whole range of experience from the first movings of God upon the heart, across the spectrum of conviction and acknowledgment, confession and forgiveness and justification, the experience of living with Christ in the heart, the secret of meeting and overcoming every temptation and so being victorious over sin. Finally, we have thought about retracing our steps back to God should we fall. We have explored all this because, as we stated at the beginning of the book, every human being must go through each and all of these steps, (which are involved with the former rain), to be right with God, and thus to be prepared to receive the latter rain. There can be no skipping at any point. To refuse any step required in the process is to make a full reconciliation and recovery impossible. But let it be said of us as Paul wrote to the Hebrews, "But we are not of those who draw back to perdition, but of those who believe to the saving of the soul" (Hebrews 10:39).

I end by repeating some of the Spirit of Prophecy statements and some of the Bible texts quoted in chapter two:

> If you are right with God today, you are ready if Christ should come today. What we need is Christ formed within, the hope of glory.[7]

> It is our work today to yield our souls to Christ, that we may be fitted for the time of refreshing from the presence of the Lord—fitted for the baptism of the Holy Spirit.[8]

> Ask the Lord for rain in the time of the latter rain. The Lord will . . . give them showers of rain (Zechariah 10:1).

> For I will pour water on him who is thirsty, and floods on the dry ground (Isaiah 44:3).

1. White, *Patriarchs and Prophets*, page 123.
2. White, *Thoughts from the Mount of Blessing*, page 51.
3. Volume 2, page 143.
4. White, *Review and Herald*, August 1, 1893.
5. White, *Mount of Blessing*, page 9.
6. White, *Our High Calling*, page 88.
7. White, *In Heavenly Places*, page 227.
8. White, *Evangelism*, page 702.